THE BOOK OF JONAH

A CENTRE FOR PENTECOSTAL THEOLOGY BIBLE STUDY

CENTRE FOR PENTECOSTAL THEOLOGY
BIBLE STUDY SERIES

Edited by
Lee Roy Martin
John Christopher Thomas

CPT Press
Cleveland, Tennessee

THE BOOK OF
JONAH

A CENTRE FOR PENTECOSTAL THEOLOGY
BIBLE STUDY

Lee Roy Martin

CPT Press
Cleveland, Tennessee

Handouts and PowerPoint presentations may be
downloaded free of charge at
http://pentecostaltheology.org under 'Resources'.

The Book of Jonah
A Centre for Pentecostal Theology Bible Study

Published by CPT Press
900 Walker ST NE
Cleveland, TN 37311
USA
email. cptpress@pentecostaltheology.org
website. www.cptpress.com

Library of Congress Control Number: 2015910592

ISBN-13: 9781935931539

Cover art by Jan Brueghel the Elder, Jonah Leaving the Fish, oil on panel, ca. 1600

Citations of Scripture are translations of the author.

For
Stephen, Michael, and Kendra

TABLE OF CONTENTS

PREFACE

This study is based upon my commentary on the book of Jonah, which is soon to be available in the *Pentecostal Commentary on the Twelve Minor Prophets*, edited by John Christopher Thomas (Blandford Forum, UK: Deo Publishing).

I offer my thanks to my good friend and colleague Chris Thomas, who invited me to write the commentary on Jonah. As always, I am indebted to the Church of God for giving me a spiritual home, to the Pentecostal Theological Seminary for giving me a place to minister, and to my family for giving me reason for living.

Jonah is an amazing little book, and I trust that you will be greatly blessed by entering the story of this stubborn prophet as he struggles against a patient and gracious God.

Lee Roy Martin
Cleveland, Tennessee
February 24, 2016

How to Use this Book

This Bible study is written for pastors and lay persons who desire to live a Spirit-filled life that is formed and directed by Holy Scripture. Although the book is presented in popular language, it is based upon the exegesis of Jonah in its original language and includes the author's own translation from the Hebrew text.

This book is appropriate both for individual readers and for group study. Therefore, the materials are grouped into two parts. Part I is the Bible study itself, and it can be enjoyed by reading straight through. Part II includes lesson outlines that can be used by a teacher or preacher, and it also supplies student handouts that can be utilized in a classroom setting. Powerpoint presentations are available to be used in conjunction with the book and may be downloaded freely from the following website: http://www.pentecostaltheology.org/Jonah.

The study is organized around the five distinct scenes within the book of Jonah. Each lesson includes quite a large amount of material. Therefore, although the course is divided into five lessons, you may find it more practical to spread each lesson over two or more class sessions.

The lessons are presented in four steps that are based on the well-known 4MAT learning process (Meaning, Content, Experiment, Creative application). These four steps are consistent with the method presented by Jackie David Johns and Cheryl Bridges Johns in their important article, 'Yielding to the Spirit: A Pentecostal Approach to Group Bible Study', *Journal of*

Pentecostal Theology 1 (1992), pp. 109-34 (Sharing Our Testimony, Searching the Scriptures, Yielding to the Spirit, and Responding to the Call).

Each step serves as a stage in the learning process, and each step also addresses the different learning styles of students. Step one is an introduction to the lesson and may include group discussion. Step two is the basic content of the Scripture lesson. Steps three and four bring the lesson to bear upon the Christian life, the Church, and the world. These can be times of discussion that provide for more extensive student participation and interaction. The teacher should be at liberty to spend as much time as necessary on each step, depending upon the needs and desires of the students. Teachers are also encouraged to create learning activities that are appropriate for the students and to their particular context.

The four learning steps may be described as follows:

1. Setting the Direction

The purpose of the first step is to get the student interested in the topic. In this step we answer the question, 'Why do we need to study this lesson?' Teachers can feel free to lead a discussion that brings to the surface the life needs of the students in relation to the lesson at hand. Initial discussions can be based upon the teacher's own context or upon the suggested Discussion Starters that are offered in the book. The overall goal is to involve the students and their personal testimonies so that they become deeply engaged in the topic at hand. The challenges faced by each student will resonate with other members of the group, and a sense of community will develop.

2. Hearing the Word of God

The second step is the basic Bible lesson and comprises the bulk of the material in this manual. Here we answer the question, 'What do we learn from this Scripture passage?'

The lesson is presented according to a Wesleyan Pentecostal approach to Scripture that recognizes the role of experience, the relationality of truth, the contextual importance of story, and the overarching guidance of the Holy Spirit. Thus, the Bible is more than a roadmap or list of principles; instead, it is God's dynamic Spirit-Word that continues to speak to God's people in new and creative ways.

3. Connecting with Jonah

The purpose of the third step is to apply the Scripture to our Churches and to our lives as Christians. We answer the question, 'How does this lesson pertain to us?' In this step, we 'Yield to the Spirit'. We must be open to the convicting power of the Holy Spirit, who will challenge, confront, and transform the believer who is hungry for God and willing to hear God's voice. The goal of Bible study is not just the acquisition of information, but that each of us is held accountable for what we hear in Scripture.

4. What if … ?

This final step is a creative process that seeks to answer the question, 'How can we build upon the foundation laid in this lesson?' In other words, the lesson serves as a base for generating new and imaginative ideas that move beyond the basic applications that are discovered in step three. How do we live in the presence of God? How do we demonstrate the love of God to the world? In light of our Bible lesson, what is God calling us to do?

For more information on teaching with the students' learning styles in mind, see Marlene D. Lefever, *Learning Styles: Reaching Everyone God Gave You to Teach* (Colorado Springs, CO: David C. Cook, 2002).

Part I

A Study of the Book of Jonah

1

A DIFFICULT ASSIGNMENT AND A DANGEROUS CHOICE: JONAH 1.1-3

Setting the Direction: Are We Willing?

I visited recently with a friend who was struggling. With great urgency in his voice and tears in his eyes he said, 'I don't know what God wants me to do. If he would just tell me what to do, I would do it. I would do whatever he tells me. I want to do God's will, but I am not hearing from God.' Like this young man, most Christians are hungry to hear from God and to learn the will of God for their lives.

Sometimes, however, God gives us an assignment that is difficult or an assignment that we simple do not want to fulfill. In those situations we are tempted to resist God's will and to continue on the path of least resistance. We may say that we want to be faithful, but it can be hard to follow through on our commitment.

At one time in my life, I spent several months praying and fasting for God's direction in regard to future ministry. During the state convention, the State Administrative Bishop asked me if I would be willing to accept a certain pastorate. The church was in financial trouble, and it had a reputation for being difficult. I could hardly believe that the Bishop was asking me to take that church; therefore, I replied that I was not interested. I was surprised a few weeks later to receive an official appointment letter in the mail. The Bishop had appointed me as pastor of the church that I had declined. I called him on the telephone and asked him to reconsider, but he refused to change the appointment. Having no options, I accepted the pastorate reluctantly, and I served as pastor for two years. Looking back on that experience, I now realize that my time at that church was exactly what the Lord wanted for me and my family. I can point to several important events that took place during those two years that contributed to the shape of my life and ministry as it is today. I was in the center of God's will, but I could not see it at the time.

Discussion Starters

Can you think of a time when you were given an assignment that you did not want to fulfill?

Perhaps you felt unqualified, or you did not agree with the assignment, or you did not think it was part of your responsibilities?

How did you respond?

Did you try to evade the boss and ignore instructions, hoping he/she would forget about it?

How did the experience make you feel?

Can you point to a time that you disobeyed God?

Why did you disobey?

How did you feel about it?

Hearing the Word of God

> ¹The Word of the LORD came to Jonah the son of Amittai, saying, ²Arise! Go to Nineveh, that great city, and call out against it, because their evil has risen up into my presence. ³And Jonah arose to flee to Tarshish from the presence of the LORD. He went down to Joppa, and he found a ship going to Tarshish. He paid its fare and he went down into it, to go with them to Tarshish from the presence of the LORD (Jonah 1.1-3).

Introduction to the Book of Jonah

Everyone knows the story of Jonah and the whale – or big fish, as the book of Jonah puts it – but this episode in the life of Jonah carries deeper significance than we sometimes realize. Jonah is a rebellious prophet who refuses to complete the assignment that the LORD gives to him. Why does Jonah run from his calling? The answer to that question gets to the heart of the message of this little book.

Overview of the Book of Jonah

Bible scholars agree that the book of Jonah is set forth in two halves, each halve being two chapters. Each of these halves begins with the same statement. 'The Word of the LORD came to Jonah' (1.1; 3.1). In the first half of the book, Jonah is at sea, and in the second half, Jonah is in Nineveh. In each half of the book Jonah encounters a group of non-Israelites who pray and turn to God. In each half of the book, Jonah prays a prayer that relates to the LORD's saving mercy. In each half of the book, God 'prepares' one of his creatures to serve as a lesson to Jonah. The two halves of the book include a number of parallels; however, the message of the story emerges from those elements that are hidden in the first half of the book but which rise to the surface in the second half. Jonah's motive for fleeing and Jonah's feelings are not revealed in the first half of the book, but they become important in the second half. Finally, in the first part of the book the LORD pursues Jonah by means of the big storm and the big fish, but in the final chapter the LORD pursues Jonah through direct personal encounter and repeated questioning. The LORD relentlessly probes the depths of Jonah's heart, and Jonah cannot escape.

Outline of the Book of Jonah

I. Jonah, the Fleeing Prophet (1.1–2.10)
    A. God speaks and Jonah flees (1.1-3)
    B. God pursues Jonah (1.4-16)
        1. The storm threatens the ship (1.4-6)
        2. Jonah confesses his disobedience (1.7-10)
        3. The sailors throw Jonah into the sea (1.11-16)
    C. God prepares a big fish (1.17-2.10)
        1. The fish swallows Jonah (1.17)
        2. Jonah gives thanks (2.1-9)
        3. The fish regurgitates Jonah onto dry land (2.10)

II. Jonah, the Obedient (but Angry) Prophet (3.1–4.11)
    A. God speaks to Jonah again (3.1-2)
    B. Jonah preaches in Nineveh (3.3-10)
        1. Nineveh repents (3.3-9)
        2. God saves Nineveh (3.10)
    C. Jonah is angry and God responds (4.1-11)
        1. The anger of Jonah (4.1-5)
        2. The mercy of God (4.6-11)

The Book of Jonah Is Different from Other Prophetic Books

Jonah Begins without a Title

Several aspects of the book of Jonah set it apart from the other prophetic books. First of all, *Jonah lacks a title*. Jonah is the only prophetic book that has no title or introduction. For example, the book of Isaiah is called 'The vision of Isaiah' (Isa. 1.1). Joel is entitled, 'The Word of the LORD that came to Joel' (Joel 1.1); Amos is designated as 'The words of Amos' (Amos 1.1); and Nahum has the heading, 'The burden of Nineveh' (Nah. 1.1).

We could also point to Jer. 1.1; Hos. 1.1; Obad. 1.1; Mic. 1.1; Hab. 1.1; Zeph. 1.1; and Mal. 1.1. Other prophetic books begin with introductions that describe the setting and date of the prophet's ministry. Zechariah, for example is prefixed with the following description. 'In the eighth month, in the second year of Darius, the Word of the LORD came to Zechariah' (Zech. 1.1; cf. Ezek. 1.1 and Hag. 1.1). Apparently, the writer does not want to delay the beginning of the story by including any unnecessary information. The story takes off from the very first word.

Jonah Is a Story

Another characteristic that makes Jonah different is that *Jonah is entirely a story about the prophet.* From beginning to end, the book of Jonah is a story. Jonah preaches one short message consisting of a single sentence (Jonah 3.4). Other prophetic books are mostly made up of prophecies, with very little space devoted to the lives of the prophets (Isaiah 7; 36–39; Jeremiah 27–28; 37–44; Amos 7.10-17). The prophets sometimes act out their messages in dramatic form (Isa. 20.2-4; Jer. 13.1-11; 18.1-12; Ezekiel 4–5; Hos. 1.2–3.5), but only the book of Jonah presents its message entirely in the form of a story about the prophet. Jonah's use of story demonstrates that God can speak to us through a variety of means. He can speak through a prophecy, sermon, a song, a drama, a parable, or a story.

Jonah Is Intense

Another unique quality of Jonah is its unceasing intensity. Most everything in Jonah is big and intense. The Hebrew word 'big' (*gadol*) is found fourteen times in the book of Jonah and is used in the following ways. Nineveh is called a *big* city (1.2); God sends a *big* wind (1.4), which causes a *big* storm (1.12); the sailors have a *big* fear (1.10); God sends a *big* fish to swallow Jonah (1.17); the *big* people (3.5) and *big* leaders repent (3.7), which causes Jonah to have a *big* anger (4.1); etc. Everything in Jonah is big and intense.

The language of Jonah is big because the message of the book is big. It is about life and death, wickedness and repentance, and the unpredictable actions of God. The story of Jonah confronts urgent and vital questions. It requires a big storm, a big fish, and the salvation of a big city to capture the big message of this little book.

Jonah Is Sent on a Foreign Mission

Unlike the mission of other prophets, Jonah's assignment requires him to travel to a foreign country where he will deliver a message of judgment. While other prophets set forth oracles against the nations (Isaiah 13–23; Jeremiah 46–50; Ezekiel 25–32; Amos 1–2; Obadiah; Nahum), they do not preach directly to the people of those nations.

Jonah Is Given a Second Commission

Jonah is the only prophet who needed to have his assignment repeated a second time. The first time that God called Jonah, he ran away from his calling. Only after he had spent three days in the belly of the great fish did Jonah decide to obey God's call and go to the city of Nineveh.

Jonah's Prophecy Omits God

Jonah is the only prophet who does not mention God in his preaching. Jonah neither begins his prophecy with the usual messenger formula, 'Thus says the LORD', nor does he conclude with the common phrase, 'declares the LORD'. It is quite unusual for a prophet to preach a message that does not make specific reference to God, but Jonah uses neither the general term 'God' (*'elohim*) nor the more specific term 'Jehovah' (in Hebrew, *Yahweh*), which is the personal name of Israel's God.

A Difficult Assignment

> ¹**The Word of the LORD came to Jonah the son of Amittai, saying ... (Jonah 1.1)**

The first half of the book (chapters 1 and 2) tells of God's assignment to Jonah and Jonah's refusal to obey. Jonah's flight can be divided into three scenes that chronicle Jonah's attempt to evade the call of God. In the first scene, we find God and Jonah on the land (1.1-3). In the second scene, we follow Jonah and the sailors on the ship (1.4-16); and in the third scene, we see Jonah and the fish in the sea (1.17–2.10).

The difficult assignment causes tension between Jonah and God.

The story of Jonah gets under way quickly. Within the first three verses we learn the identity of the main characters (God and Jonah); we discover the event that triggers the story (Jonah's call to Nineveh); and we observe the conflict that moves the story along (Jonah's resistance to God).

Jonah's Assignment comes by the Word of the LORD.

The coming of the prophetic 'word' (*davar*) is a powerful revelatory experience in the life of a prophet. It is an encounter with the majesty and holiness of God. The coming of the Word of the LORD is a transforming encounter in which the prophet is enabled to view reality from the perspective of God himself. 'My thoughts are not your thoughts, and your ways are not my ways', says the LORD (Isa. 55.8), but when the Word of the LORD *happens*, the prophet is made to think God's thoughts, adopt God's ways, and feel God's passions. Moses was transformed when the LORD appeared to him in the burning bush (Exod. 3.2). Samuel was just a boy, but he became a powerful prophet of revival when the LORD spoke to him by night (1 Sam. 3.4-21). Isaiah was transformed by his encounter with the holy God (Isa. 6.1-8). Amos declared that he was neither a prophet nor the son of a prophet, but 'the LORD God has spoken; who can help but prophesy' (Amos 3.8). Jeremiah experienced the life changing call to be a prophet and he asserted that the prophetic word was like 'burning fire shut up' in his bones (Jer. 20.9) and like a 'hammer that breaks a rock in pieces' (Jer. 23.29).

The Word of the LORD is sometimes visual. 'The word that Isaiah son of Amoz saw concerning Judah and Jerusalem' (Isa. 2.1); 'But which of them has stood in the council of the LORD to see or to hear his word?' (Jer. 23.18). Therefore, the 'Word of the LORD' can come through the means of a vision – 'Afterwards, the Word of the LORD came to Abram in a vision.

Fear not, Abram. I am your shield and your very great reward' (Gen. 15.1) or a dream – 'When a prophet of the LORD is among you, I will reveal myself to him in visions and I will speak to him in dreams' (Num. 12.6).

The Word of the LORD is more than speech or conversation; it is an event. The prophets are not described as 'hearing' the word; rather, the Word of the LORD 'comes' to them or 'happens' to them. The Hebrew verb in this verse (*hayah*) means also 'to happen', 'to occur'. Therefore, the phrase 'the Word of the LORD *happened* to Jonah' or '*occurred* to Jonah' suggests an event, an encounter with God.

The Word of the LORD is not Jonah's word; it is God's Word. The Word does not originate in Jonah, and he does not own it or control it. He cannot change it. This is an important point for preachers, teachers, and all Spirit-filled Christians. We do not manufacture the Word of the LORD; we can not change it, and we must not ignore it.

Like Jonah, we may be recipients of the Word of the LORD. Since the Day of Pentecost, the Church has been a Spirit-filled prophetic community that proclaims the message of Jesus. Pentecost is a fulfillment of Joel 2.28 that says, 'In the last days, says God, I will pour out my Spirit on all people. Your sons and daughters will prophesy, your young men will see visions, your old men will dream dreams. On my men servants and women servants, I will pour out my Spirit in those days, and they will prophesy' (Acts 2.17-18).

The Assignment is Given to Jonah

Who is Jonah? The main character of the book and recipient of the Word of the LORD is Jonah, the son of Amittai. The name 'Jonah' ('dove') symbolizes gentleness and beauty (Song 5.2) and timidity (Hos. 11.11). Also, the dove is a sacrificial animal brought to the tabernacle as a sin offering (Lev. 12.6).

'Amittai' means 'true' or 'faithful'; therefore, Jonah's name suggests that he might be a gentle, timid, but faithful prophet and that perhaps he will offer himself on behalf of others.

Jonah was an experienced prophet. His name identifies him as the eighth century prophet who predicted God's merciful salvation of Israel through the leadership of king Jeroboam II. The Scripture tells us the story of Jonah's earlier prophecy:

> [Jeroboam] was the one who restored the boundaries of Israel from Lebo Hamath to the Sea of the Arabah, in accordance with the Word of the LORD, the God of Israel, which was spoken through his servant Jonah son of Amittai, the prophet of Gath Hepher. The LORD saw how bitterly everyone in Israel, slave or free, was suffering; and there was no one to save them. And since the LORD had not said he would blot out the name of Israel from under heaven, he saved them by the hand of Jeroboam son of Jehoash (2 Kgs 14.25-27).

Jonah preached grace to a wicked king. Although Jeroboam was a wicked king, God graciously came to his aid in order to save Israel from her suffering and to prevent her from being totally destroyed. At the same time that Hosea and Amos were rebuking Israel with messages of judgment, Jonah was known as a prophet of grace and salvation.

Jonah's Assignment Is to Go to Nineveh

²Arise! Go to Nineveh, that great city, and call out against it, because their evil has risen up into my presence (Jonah 1.2).

Nineveh is a major city in the Assyrian Empire and a bitter enemy of Israel. The Assyrians were a major source of Israel's suffering, beginning when Adad-Nirari III invaded Palestine in the days of Joash (Jeroboam's father), and continuing when the Assyrian rulers invaded the area five times between 773 and 754.

Although God spares Nineveh for a time, he would later execute complete judgment upon the wicked city. Reveling in Nineveh's demise, the prophet Nahum writes, 'Woe to the bloody city, full of lies and booty' (Nah. 3.1).

Nineveh is the enemy, but Nineveh is not the real point of the story. Historical details appear to be purposefully omitted. For example, the year of Jonah's mission is not reported; the name of Israel's king is not given; and the name of Nineveh's king is not mentioned. In fact, no human actor is named in the book except Jonah. Furthermore, Jonah's journey to the distant city is entirely omitted, and few details are provided about his visit to the city.

What is most important in the book of Jonah is the response by both God and Jonah to the repentance of Nineveh. Consequently, the story focuses on God's compassionate response to Israel's wicked enemy and Jonah's sense of displeasure toward God's change of heart.

The LORD commands Jonah to 'arise, and go' to the big city of Nineveh and 'cry out' against it because of its evil. The Assyrians were known for their cruelty and violence, so Jonah would not have been surprised that Nineveh would be described as a 'evil' city. That the wickedness of Nineveh has reached up to God is reminiscent of Sodom and Gomorrah (Gen. 18.21), and evokes a sense of impending doom.

The cries of the prophets are usually directed against the sins of Israel. For example, Isaiah writes, 'Declare to my people their rebellion and to the house of Jacob their sins' (Isa. 58.1), and Jeremiah says, 'The LORD said to me, Speak forth all these words in the towns of Judah and in the streets of Jerusalem' Jer. 11.6). Jonah, however, does not preach to Israel. Instead, he becomes the first prophet who is commanded to travel to a foreign people and rebuke them for their wickedness.

A Dangerous Decision

> ³**And Jonah arose to flee to Tarshish from the presence of the LORD. He went down to Joppa, and he found a ship going to Tarshish. He paid its fare and he went down into it, to go with them to Tarshish from the presence of the LORD (Jonah 1.3).**

For some reason, Jonah decides to disregard the clear command that God had given him. In an attempt to escape the 'presence of the LORD', he flees westward toward Tarshish instead of going eastward to Nineveh. Jonah the 'dove' is not as faithful and submissive as his name might indicate.

Although God lays upon his prophets a powerful calling, he does not force them into compliance. He allows his prophets the freedom to disobey, and sometimes they resist the will of God. Because of the heavy burden of the prophetic calling, virtually every prophet offers initial resistance. The message that is carried by the prophet is called a 'burden'. For example, Isa. 13.1, 'The burden concerning Babylon, which Isaiah the son of Amoz saw'; Nah. 1.1, 'The burden concerning Nineveh. The book of the vision of Nahum the Elkoshite'; Hab. 1.1, 'The burden which Habakkuk the prophet saw'. The prophetic ministry is challenging, demanding, and sometimes heartbreaking.

Jonah resists his assignment, but that does not mean that he takes God lightly. He has encountered God, and he must face the seriousness of the prophetic call. A prophet cannot pretend that the Word of the LORD does not exist. God is a real presence whose word demands a response; and Jonah's response was to flee. Like Jonah, Pentecostals carry with them the constant conviction that the word of God really matters, that God is present, and that God demands our full attention. Jonah is right to take God seriously.

Jonah not only resists his assignment, he refuses to talk to God. While it is right to take God seriously, it is wrong to clam up and shut out God from our lives. The first chapter of Jonah demonstrates that stubborn silence and continued disobedience to the will of God results only in suffering to ourselves and to all who are around us.

No other prophet refused their assignment like Jonah. Other prophets resisted God initially, but no other prophet turned and ran away. Moses resisted his commission on the grounds that he was not an eloquent speaker – 'But Moses said to the LORD, Oh, my LORD, I am not eloquent, neither in the past nor since you have spoken to your servant; but I am slow of speech and of tongue' (Exod. 4.10). Gideon objected to the summons from God because his family was insignificant – 'And he said to Him, O LORD, how shall I deliver Israel? My family is the least in Manasseh, and I am the youngest in my father's house' (Judg. 6.15). Jeremiah cited his youth as reason enough to protest God's call – 'Then I said, Ah, Lord GOD! Truly I do not know how to speak, because I am just a boy' (Jer. 1.6). These prophets challenged God initially; but, in the end, they surrendered themselves to the will of God. Isaiah, for example, finally cried out 'Here am I; send me!' (Isa. 6.8).

Other prophets offer objections, but Jonah does not protest. Other prophets wrestle with God, but Jonah does not wrestle. Instead, Jonah flees. The LORD had trusted Jonah enough to send him to Nineveh, but Jonah does not trust God enough to obey God and go to Nineveh.

It seems that Jonah quickly found a ship that would take him away from his assignment. Jonah learned that disobedience comes easily for the one whose heart is rebellious – as the great preacher Charles Spurgeon once said, 'The way to hell is downhill'.

Jonah's flight is highlighted in verse 3 by the repetition of the phrases 'to Tarshish' and 'from the presence of the LORD'. The phrase 'to Tarshish' is found in lines one, three, and five; and the phrase 'from the presence of the LORD' concludes both the first line and the last line. The repetition and placement of the phrases 'to Tarshish' and 'from the presence of the LORD' draw attention to Jonah's radical choice to flee from God.

Tarshish was as far from Nineveh as Jonah could go. According to Isaiah, Tarshish as a faraway place that has not heard of the LORD's fame or his glory – 'And I will set a sign among them and will send survivors from them to the nations. Tarshish, Put, Lud, Meshech, Rosh, Tubal, and Javan, to the distant coastlands that have neither heard my fame nor seen my glory' (Isa. 66.19). Isaiah is pointing to a location near the edge of the world as it was known to Jonah. As a faraway place on the Mediterranean sea, it was located in the opposite direction from Nineveh.

Why did Jonah make this dangerous choice to flee from his prophetic assignment? He must have had a strong reason for giving up his prophetic ministry and running to a city where he would have no friends or family. At this point, however, Jonah's motive is not stated; and the suspense builds until we reach a sudden turning point in chapter 4. At this point we can only speculate as to Jonah's motives. Is the distance too far? Nineveh lies some 700 miles east of Israel; but distance cannot be Jonah's reason because Tarshish is even farther away. Is it fear of being contaminated by the Gentiles? If so, then why does Jonah join himself to a gentile crew on a ship bound for a pagan city. Can it be the dangers of travel? Surely not, since a journey on the well traveled roads to Nineveh could hardly be more dangerous than a sea voyage to the far corners of the world. It appears that Jonah's dangerous choice is entirely irrational and so must be based on deep and powerful reasons that we can not yet discern. We know one thing, however. We know that Jonah is fleeing from God, a strange action indeed for a man of God.

Whatever Jonah's reasons may have been, they were nothing more than 'excuses'. We also know how to invent various excuses for not obeying the clear commands of God, but he does not honor our flimsy excuses.

Can Jonah escape the presence of God? Of course not. Jonah would certainly be aware of the Psalmist's great confession.

> Where can I go from your Spirit? Or where can I flee from your presence? If I go up to heaven, you are there; if I make my bed in *sheol*, behold, you are there. If I take the wings of the morning, if I dwell in the farthest part of the sea, even there your hand will lead me, and your right hand will hold me (Ps. 139.7-10; cf. Jer. 23.24 and Amos 9.1-3).

Conclusion

Jonah was given a difficult assignment, and he chose to disobey. We too are faced with difficult choices. Sometimes the Word of God challenges us in ways that seem beyond our ability. God may ask us to venture outside of our comfort zone in order to stretch us and teach us. Whenever we feel like God is calling us to do more than we are able, we should express our reservations to him in earnest prayer. Unlike Jonah, we should not be silent and we should not flee from the presence of God. The presence of God is our shelter, our refuge, and our strength.

Connecting with Jonah

(Questions for discussion)

How does God deliver the 'Word of the LORD' to the Church today?

Which gifts of the Spirit (including prophecy) do you see being exercised in the Church?

Can you share an experience when you attempted to escape an assignment from God?

What kinds of excuses have you given for not obeying God?

How do we joyously speak forth the good news of God's grace?

Do you ever avoid talking to God because you are afraid of what he may ask you to do for him?

Are you willing to minister to a foreign people? Are you willing to minister to your neighbor? Are you willing to minister to your family?

How do we overcome our areas of resistance to God's will?

What if ... ?

(Creative and imaginative ideas)

What if we identify and list the people that we care about the least, then go and share the Gospel with them?

What if we find a Scripture that is very difficult for us to obey, then begin to practice it this very day?

What if we would take the time to visit a nursing home?

What if we volunteer for work at a food bank, soup kitchen, or homeless shelter?

Now, come up with your own 'What if ... ?'

2

DISOBEDIENCE AND ITS STORMY EFFECTS: JONAH 1.4-16

Setting the Direction: Dangers of Disobedience

Broken families, divorce, strife, financial ruin, poverty, traumatized children, etc. – these are the tragic effects of our abuse of human freedom. Our destructive behavior would not be so bad if it harmed only ourselves, but our behavior affects everyone around us. Scripture tells us that 'We do not live to ourselves, and we do not die to ourselves' (Rom. 14.7). We live in families that are dramatically affected by our every action, whether or not we can see those effects immediately. The family is so closely connected that the husband and wife are said to be 'one flesh' (Gen. 2.24). Furthermore, we are members of the body of Christ, and the actions of one member affect the entire body (1 Cor. 5.1-8 and 12.12-26). Finally, we are citizens in the world at large, and as Christians we should be manifesting the Kingdom of God in the earth (1 Pet. 3.8-18).

Discussion Starters

How did the behavior of your parents affect you for good or for bad?

Can you name a specific action taken by another person that affected you dramatically?

Can you name a specific choice that you have made that affected others in a negative way?

When you make decisions, do you consider the affects that your decision might have on other people?

Hearing the Word of God

Introduction

In the previous lesson, God speaks to Jonah the prophet and calls him to a difficult foreign mission. Jonah's assignment is to go and preach to the evil city of Nineveh, a terrible enemy of Israel. For some reason, however, Jonah refuses to go. Instead he flees toward the distant city of Tarshish. In this lesson we follow Jonah as he attempts to escape the presence of the LORD. Jonah's choice to flee is a dangerous decision.

Disobedience Brings Stormy Effects

⁴But the LORD hurled a great wind upon the sea, so a great tempest came in the sea, and the ship was threatened to be broken apart. ⁵The mariners were afraid, and every man cried out to his god. And they hurled the cargo that was in the ship into the sea, to make it lighter for them. Meanwhile Jonah had gone down into the recesses of the ship; he had lain down, and he was sound asleep (Jonah 1.4-5) .

Jonah is on his way to Tarshish, and he thinks he has gotten away from his assignment, but God is in pursuit of the fleeing prophet. God hurls a mighty wind (*ruach*) that stirs up a raging storm, and the ship is in danger of sinking. The contrast here is between the tempestuous sea, which represents the anger of God as he pursues his fleeing prophet, and the slumber of Jonah, who is apparently unfazed, unfeeling, and apathetic. He is trying to forget God, but God will not be forgotten. Jonah may be asleep, but God is awake, and he is shaking Jonah.

The power of God can create and the power of God can destroy. The LORD sends the wind (*ruach*) over the sea, which brings to mind the Spirit (*ruach*) of God that moves over the waters of creation (Gen. 1.2). In Genesis, the movement of *ruach* is an act of creation, but here in Jonah the *ruach* stirs the waters into a raging and potentially destructive storm. Several places in Scripture, the word 'tempest' (*sa'ar*) is used as a symbol of God's anger and judgment (Jer. 23.19; Isa. 29.6).

The storm is God's way of confronting Jonah with his disobedience. Since Jonah refuses to talk to God, the storm is God's method of communication. Have you considered that the storm in your life may have been created by God himself? Is God trying to get your attention? Throughout Scripture, God finds a multitude of ways to discipline and confront his erring children. For example, a disobedient prophet was killed by a lion because he had disobeyed God's directives (1 Kgs 13.7-32). Can you think of other places in Scripture where God confronts people with their disobedience? (Examples: The Israelites are punished several times in the wilderness; Moses is refused entry into the Promised Land; Samson is captured by the Philistines; David is confronted by Nathan in 2 Samuel 12; Nebuchadnezzar is turned into a madman; Rehoboam has his kingdom divided; Herod is eaten with worms; Ananias and Sapphira are struck dead; and there are many others.)

Jonah's disobedience endangers not only himself but also the sailors and their ship. The crew of the ship are terrified by the storm and they cry out to their gods for help. When the situation does not get any better, they begin throwing everything overboard in order to lighten the ship. A lighter ship is easier to steer in a storm. It is clear that our disobedience to God results in misery and suffering not only to ourselves but also to others.

Jonah, however, is not yet suffering – he is asleep. He had gone down below deck to the remotest part of the ship, and had fallen into a deep sleep. The ship is here called a *sefinah*, which is a large vessel with a deck. Therefore, the meaning of this verse is that Jonah had gone below deck; and he had sought out a place where he could be free from contact with the sailors. Apparently, Jonah wished to be isolated from both God and humans. The 'remotest part' may also foreshadow his later experience in the belly of the great fish and his desire to die, since the 'remotest part' (*yerikah*) can be used to describe the depths of the pit of death (Isa. 14.15; Ezek. 32.23).

People in trouble often avoid the very things that can help them to move toward recovery. Do we avoid prayer when we are disobedient? Do we avoid church attendance and Christian fellowship when we have been unfaithful?

Disobedience Rebuked

⁶The captain of the ship approached and said to him, 'Why are you sleeping? Arise, cry out to your God. Perhaps God will consider us, and we will not perish' (Jonah 1.6).

The ship is in danger, but Jonah sleeps. The captain of the ship does not understand how Jonah can sleep through the storm. He asks Jonah, 'What are you doing asleep?'. The Hebrew phrase *mah-leka* implies displeasure and is often translated, 'What is wrong with you?' (Gen. 21.17). For example, when Elijah flees to the wilderness, the LORD comes to him with the question, 'What are you doing here?' (1 Kgs 19.9). The ship's crew had been crying out to their gods, and the captain rebukes Jonah, saying, 'Arise, cry out to your God'. It seems that God is using an unbeliever to speak to Jonah the prophet. How does God do the same for us?

Jonah was sleeping during a time of confusion – the sailors were running to and fro trying to save the ship. Everyone was praying except Jonah. In times of confusion, every believer should be awake and praying. Jesus rebuked his disciples say-ing, 'Could you not watch with me one hour?' (Mt. 26.40).

Jonah was sleeping during a time of great danger – the ship was likely to sink. The storm was raging, but still Jonah slept. All about us souls are dying – do we sleep? Our families are struggling – are we asleep? We are living in 'perilous times' (2 Tim. 3.1) – we must be awake and praying.

Jonah was sleeping when he should have been awake. Of all people, he should have been awake and praying. How can Jonah sleep through the dashing of the waves, the howling of the winds, the straining of the timbers, the lurching of the ship, and the shouting of the sailors? How can we sleep while the world cries out, while nations rage, while guns roar, while children cry, while the aged die alone?

Our times require a praying church. Our times demand a church that is full of the Holy Spirit and power. The world needs the prayers of Christians; seekers need direction; hurting people need healing; new converts need to be established; workers need to be trained; the Gospel needs to be preached. We must not retreat and escape from reality. We must not lie down and fall asleep!

The captain pleads with Jonah to pray, but Jonah did not pray. The captain says, 'Perhaps your god will give a thought to us and we will not perish'. The captain hopes that God will give his attention to their plight, but the truth is that God has already given 'a thought' to Jonah. In fact, the storm exists precisely because God is thinking of Jonah.

Disobedience Revealed

> [7] And they said to each other, 'Come; let us cast lots, that we may know who is the cause of our calamity'. So they cast lots, and the lot fell on Jonah. [8] Then they said to him, 'Please tell us, who is the cause of our calamity? What is your business? Where do you come from? What is your country? Who is your people?' [9] And he said to them, 'I am a Hebrew; and I fear the LORD, the God of heaven, who made the sea and the dry land'. [10] Then the men feared greatly, and said to him, 'What have you done?' For the men knew that he had fled from the presence of the LORD, because he had told them (Jonah 1.7-10).

While the captain is busy rebuking the prophet, the ship's crew decides to cast lots in an effort to determine the cause of the storm. They assume (and rightly so) that someone on the ship has incurred the wrath of God and that the storm is a divine judgment against that person. The casting of lots was a conventional way to discern God's will in situations where decisions must be made or guilt must be determined. A proverb says, 'The lot is cast into the lap, but the whole decision is from the LORD' (Prov. 16.33, cf. Lev. 16.8; Num. 26.55). When the lots are cast, Jonah is identified as the guilty party.

The crew fire a volley of questions at Jonah, in order to learn more about the reasons for the storm. They ask, 'What is your business? Where do you come from? What is your country? Who is your people?' Jonah has been caught. His disobedience has been revealed. It reminds me of the Scripture that says, 'be sure your sin will find you out' (Num. 32.23).

Under pressure from the sailors, Jonah replies, 'I am a Hebrew, and the LORD the God of heaven and earth do I fear, who made the sea and the dry land'. Jonah seems willing to speak *about* God but still he is unwilling to speak *to* God. Jonah's answer to the sailors is true and apparently honest, but it lacks any real explanation of the situation. Jonah is hiding his feelings. We would like to see Jonah fall down and repent of his disobedience. We would hope that Jonah would sincerely apologize to the sailors for causing them such harm and loss.

Jonah's statement of faith, in spite of its brevity, is important in its content. Jonah confesses that the LORD rules as God over more than Israel; he is 'God of heaven and earth'; he is God over these sailors and over this ship. Jonah proclaims that the LORD is God over the sea and the land, since he created them both. The sea and the storm that is in the sea are in the LORD's control.

After Jonah says that he fears the LORD we read that the sailors 'feared greatly'; literally, 'they feared a great fear'. It is ironic that even though they do not serve the LORD, their fear of him is 'great', while the prophet, who claims to serve the

LORD, does not fear 'greatly'. Their great fear is caused by the revelation that Jonah is fleeing from the presence of the LORD.

Jonah's conversation with the sailors both begins and ends with the verb 'tell' (*nagid*). The sailors say to Jonah, 'Tell us …' (1.8), and the conversation concludes with the words, 'he had told them' (1.10). Jonah tells the sailors; why does he refuse to tell the LORD?

Are there times when we talk to people, but we do not talk to God? We may tell our friends; we may tell our pastor; we may tell our counselor; we may tell our parents; we may tell our children; we may tell our spouse; but we are walking in darkness if we do not tell everything to God.

Disobedience Punished

¹¹Then said they to him, 'What must we do to you, that the sea may quiet down for us?', for the sea intensified its raging. ¹²And he said to them, 'Pick me up, and hurl me into the sea; and the sea will quiet down for you; for I know that because of me this great tempest is against you'. ¹³But the men rowed hard to return to the dry land, yet they could not, for the sea intensified its raging against them. ¹⁴And they cried out to the LORD, and said, 'Please, O the LORD, please do not let us perish for taking this man's life, and do not charge us with innocent blood; for you, O the LORD, have done as you have pleased'. ¹⁵And they picked up Jonah and hurled him into the sea; and the sea stopped its raging. ¹⁶Then the men feared the LORD greatly, and they offered a sacrifice to the LORD, and they vowed vows (Jonah 1.11-16).

Jonah confessed that he is the cause of the storm; therefore, the ship's crew ask him, 'What must we do to you that the sea may be quiet for us?' They believe that Jonah, the person who caused the storm, must know how to calm the storm as well.

Immediate action is called for, since the sea is growing more dangerous with every passing moment.

Without hesitation Jonah replies, 'Pick me up and hurl me into the sea, and the sea will quiet down for you'. He confirms the decision of the lots – his disobedience caused the tempest – and he offers, without any sign of emotion, to give up his life in order to save the ship and crew. It is important that Jonah does not volunteer to leap or dive into the sea, for that would be suicide, an act that is strictly forbidden to the Jews. Instead he asks to be lifted up (*nasaʾ*) and thrown into the deep, thus assuring that he is innocent in the matter of his death. At the same time, he is forcing the crew to bear the burden of guilt. The storm is Jonah's doing, but he is asking the sailors to deal with it. Jonah will not take responsibility for solving his own problem.

Do we realize that other people share in the consequences of our actions? We must learn to take responsibility for our own actions. We must deal with our problems and not push them off onto someone else. Paul tells us that every one must carry their own load (Gal. 6.5).

Jonah knows that he would perish if he were cast into the sea, and the fact that he is ready to die shows how serious he is about his disobedience. He refuses to go to Nineveh at any cost. Jonah is willing to die *in* his rebellion, but he is not willing to die *to* his rebellion. The prophets usually faced death in their visionary beginnings of ministry, because to see God is to die (Gen. 32.30; Exod. 33.20; Isaiah 6; etc.). To encounter God in the prophetic call is to surrender one's life, or at the least to continue life with one foot on earth and the other in the throne room of God (Isa. 6.5). God's call for Jonah to go to Nineveh, therefore, was an invitation to lay down his life on God's terms, but Jonah is determined to surrender his life only on his own terms. Jonah continues to be stubborn, even in the face of a life-threatening storm.

Even though Jonah asks the sailors to cast him overboard, they are unwilling to do so without first waging a renewed battle against the wind and waves. They row with all their might, attempting to return to the dry land, but their efforts are un-successful because the storm continues to intensify. The He-brew word translated 'return' (*shuv*) often signifies a return to God in repentance; and here the sailors are unable physically to return (*shuv*) to dry land because Jonah had not spiritually re-turned (*shuv*) to the LORD. Often, we find that God will not move to deliver us from our troubles until we turn to him with all our heart.

The sailors quickly realize that they will be unable to reach the shore, and they cry out, 'Please, the LORD, please do not let us perish for taking this man's life, and do not lay upon us in-nocent blood'. Even though Jonah is the cause of the sailors' misfortune, they are reluctant to cast him into the sea. By tak-ing Jonah on board their ship, they are obligated to protect his life even at the threat of their own. To heave a passenger over-board would be an outrageous breach of maritime law. Conse-quently, they plead with the LORD that he will not lay upon them the responsibility for Jonah's death. Their concern for Jonah makes them appear to be more righteous than Jonah. This is the first time in the story that the sailors (or anyone else for that matter) have spoken to the LORD. Having learned that it is the LORD whom Jonah has offended, the mariners plead with the LORD instead of with their own gods. It is ironic that the prophet stands by silently while the pagan sailors pray to the prophet's God.

The sailors give up their efforts to save Jonah. They pick up (*nasa'*) the prophet and hurl (*tul*) him into the water. Just as the LORD's hurling of the wind onto the sea generated the tempest, the crew's hurling of Jonah onto the sea caused the sea to stop its 'raging' (*za'af*), a rage that symbolizes the anger of the LORD (Mic. 7.9). Apparently, the casting of Jonah into the sea is un-derstood by both Jonah and the sailors as an execution for crimes against the LORD.

As soon as the sea calmed down, the mariners 'feared the LORD greatly' (cf. v. 10); they offered a sacrifice to the LORD and they vowed vows, devout responses that would be typical of a Hebrew believer and that indicate the sailors' apparent conversion to Jonah's God. We might be reminded of other non-Israelites who apparently turn to the LORD. the widow of Zarephath (1 Kgs 17.9-21) and Naaman the Syrian (2 Kgs 5.1-19). These final comments about the sailors suggest that their conduct and attitudes throughout the story are more appropriate (more righteous?) than the conduct and attitudes of Jonah. The hypocrisy of Jonah is highlighted by the behavior of the sailors. It seems that we are being challenged to emulate these non-Israelite sailors rather than the Israelite prophet.

Conclusion

Jonah's disobedience to God brought about a storm in his life that threatened not only Jonah but also those around him. In spite of the storm, Jonah continued stubbornly to resist God even to the point of dying in his rebellion. While the sailors called out to the LORD for help, the fleeing prophet kept silent and never prayed.

Up to this point in the story, Jonah has not behaved in an exemplary manner at all. He runs from his calling; he resists God's will; he does not pray; and he shows no sign of remorse.

Connecting with Jonah

(Questions for discussion)

What are some ways that we stubbornly resist God, even when he is trying to point us in the right direction?

When God disciplines me, what are the 'big storms' that he uses to get my attention?

In what ways has my disobedience negatively affected my family and my Church?

Are there times when we talk to people about our feelings, but we do not talk to God?

How does sanctification effect a change in our willingness to obey God?

Are there areas of my life that I stubbornly refuse to submit to God?

How might our disobedience harm the body of Christ?

How does God discipline a disobedient Church?

How might the disobedience of the Church bring harm to the community and the world?

When storms come our way, how can we determine if they are disciplinary actions or if they are attacks of the enemy who has purposed to destroy us?

What if ... ?

(Creative and imaginative ideas)

> What if we make a list of the people that have suffered from our disobedience, then go and apologize to them and ask for their prayers?

> What if identify ways that we are resisting God, and plan specific ways that we will remedy the situation?

> What if we would take time to pray about our sanctification?

> What if we find a way to improve the circumstances of someone who is close to us (family, friend, or neighbor)?

> Now, come up with your own 'What if ... ?'

3

A BIG FISH AND A SONG OF PRAISE: JONAH 1.17-2.10

Setting the Direction: God Seeks the Lost

My son Stephen was not in the house nor was he in the yard. Only a few minutes earlier his mother had severely rebuked him for some misbehavior. Something told me that he had run away, so I got in the car and drove around town in search of the eight-year-old prodigal. I found him a couple of miles away, riding his bike. I asked him if he had any money, and he answered, 'No'. I inquired about his plans for the night, and he admitted that he really had no plans at all. I invited him to come home with me, and he sheepishly abandoned his life on the run.

Children sometimes run away from home – usually because they had a sharp disagreement with a parent. Anger produces unwise decisions that are later regretted. And just as surely as children will run away, parents will search diligently for those children.

Similarly, we sometimes run from God; and like a good parent, God goes out in search of us. Even after we go astray, even after we flee from him, God does not discard us and replace us with someone else. God could give up on us – let us wander, let us sulk, leave us to our self-centered existence. But

God's grace persists – calling, saving, calling again, leading, teaching, confronting – always in tough and unrelenting compassion.

Furthermore, God in his pursuit is pressing us towards sanctification. Resistance is by no means unusual for those who hear the voice of God calling them to sacrificial service. Testimonies by ministers and missionaries often include talk of 'running' from the call and of 'surrender' to the call. Submission to the will and call of God is ultimately a matter of sanctification and joyful obedience. God pursues us and presses us toward sanctification. He has a way of working us into a corner where we cannot escape from his presence.

Discussion Starters

What do we do when we know that we have been caught? – when we cannot run any longer? – when we are forced into a corner by God?

How do we respond when we have gone astray and made mess of things, and now we must face the music?

Hearing the Word of God

Introduction

In the first episode of this story (Jonah 1.1-3), God speaks to Jonah the prophet and calls him to a difficult foreign mission. Jonah's assignment is to go and preach to the evil city of Nineveh, a terrible enemy of Israel. For some reason, however, Jonah refuses to go. Instead he flees toward the distant city of Tarshish. Jonah's choice to flee is a dangerous decision.

In the second episode (Jonah 1.4-16), Jonah's disobedience results in a powerful storm that places innocent bystanders in danger. Jonah then stubbornly refuses to pray and talk to God. Even in the face of God's judgment, Jonah is unwilling to submit to the will of God. At the end of the episode, Jonah is thrown into the sea and the storm abates.

In this third episode of Jonah's story, we learn of the three-day ordeal of Jonah within the belly of the fish (1.17–2.10).

Nine of its eleven verses are taken up with Jonah's song of thanksgiving, which reflects on his near-death experience. When Jonah is heaved overboard by the sailors, he strikes the water with the expectation that he will drown; but to his surprise, God sends a big fish that swallows him and thus saves him from drowning. After three days in the belly of the fish, God commands the fish to regurgitate Jonah onto the dry land; and the fish obeys the Word of the LORD.

A Surprising Deliverance

¹⁷And the LORD prepared a great fish to swallow Jonah. And Jonah was in the stomach of the fish three days and three nights (Jonah 1.17).

With verse 17, the scene shifts back to Jonah. The episode regarding the storm is now over, and the story of the sailors is also over. We pick up the story of Jonah and find him in the sea, where he sinks toward watery execution. However, since the death of Jonah is not the LORD'S objective, he prepares a big fish to swallow Jonah, and to prevent him from drowning. Jonah may *think* that God is out to kill him, but God is out to *save* Jonah, not *kill* him (God's discipline is sometimes painful – see Hebrews 12). The arrival of the fish is not a fluke of nature – it is not accidental but providential – as the word 'prepared' makes evident. Even though Jonah is running from God, doing everything he can to avoid the presence of God, God pursues him. God seeks out Jonah and will not allow him to escape. Jonah's story shows that in the face of rebellion God's grace pursues his servants and persists in calling them to mission. God's grace will find us, wherever we may be.

Jonah is in the stomach of the fish for the period of three days and three nights. Is there a meaning to the time frame of three days? In the Old Testament, one day represents a very short time (Ezra 10.13; Isa. 47.9; 66.8), while three days points to a more protracted period. Three days is not lengthy (Gen. 40.12-19), but it is time sufficient for a visit (Judg. 19.4), for making preparations for battle (Josh. 1.11) or for reaching an important decision (1 Kgs 12.5). When used in reference to a journey, three days is considered quite a long trek, especially if no food and water are taken along (Exod. 15.22). Three days without food and water, therefore, approaches the limit of human endurance (1 Sam. 30.12; Est. 4.16). In other ancient Near Eastern literature three days is the time required to travel to the underworld of death. In light of the biblical and ancient Near Eastern usage, hearers of Jonah might understand the three days and three nights in two ways. (1) as a severe taxing of Jonah's physical endurance, and (2) as the time required for the fish to rescue Jonah from the depths of the netherworld (cf. his use of '*sheol*', 2.2; and 'the pit', 2.7). In more ways than one, Jonah's confinement in the fish for 'three days and three nights' underscores the harshness of his ordeal from both a physical and emotional perspective.

Depending upon the context, the word 'stomach' (*ma'ah*) can mean literally the 'intestines' (2 Sam. 20.10), 'stomach' (Ezek. 3.3), 'reproductive organs' (Gen. 15.4; Ruth 1.11), or 'abdomen' (Dan. 2.32). It can represent figuratively the emotions (Isa. 16.11) and the affections (Ps. 40.8). The fish is Jonah's captor, whose stomach is a miserable and menacing dungeon. While it is true that the fish saves Jonah from drowning, the fish itself is only a slightly less threatening environment than the open sea.

Deliverance Produces Thanksgiving

¹And Jonah prayed to the LORD his God from the stomach of the fish, ²and he said,

I cried out because of my affliction
    unto the LORD and he heard me;
from the belly of *sheol* I cried;
    you heard my voice.
³You threw me into the deep,
    in the heart of the seas;
and a current was surrounding me;
    all your breakers and your waves passed over me.
⁴And as for me, I said,
    'I am driven from your presence;

yet I will look again upon your holy temple'.
⁵Waters enclosed me to my life.
   The deep surrounded me;
   weeds wrapped around my head.
⁶To the foundations of the mountains I descended;
   the earth, her bars closed behind me for ever;
But you brought up my life from the pit,
   Lord my God.
⁷When my life weakened within me,
   It was the Lord I remembered.
And my prayer came in to you,
   into your holy temple.
⁸They that regard worthless vanities
   abandon their covenant loyalty.
⁹But I, with a thankful voice,
   I will sacrifice to you.
What I have vowed, I will fulfill.
   Salvation is of the Lord (Jonah 2.1-9).

At last Jonah speaks to God. After three days in the belly of the fish, Jonah is ready to call upon God; he is ready to pray. The storm did not provoke Jonah to pray. The sailors could not force Jonah to pray; but from the stomach of the great fish, Jonah prays.

We expect to hear Jonah crying out to the LORD for help; but instead, we hear a prayer of thanksgiving that reports Jonah's cries after the fact. It is reported that the sailors, when threatened by the storm, 'cried out' to God (1.5, 14), and when Jonah is overwhelmed by the suffocating flood, we would expect to hear the words, 'Jonah cried out to the LORD', but no such report is to be found. Once again Jonah's deep passions are unexpressed in the narrative and withheld from the hearer of the story. Furthermore, inasmuch as the Hebrews often voiced their cries through prayers of lament, we expect Jonah to present his cries in that form. In the prayer of lament, the seeker addresses God directly and sets forth a troubling situation from which the seeker pleads to be delivered. After pleading for help, the seeker confesses faith in God and promises to praise God after deliverance has been accomplished. Examples of the lament are Psalms 3, 13, 14, 17, 22, 25, 26, and 54. Jonah, for example, might have prayed, 'Hear my cry, O God' (Ps. 61.1); 'Save me, O God' (Ps. 69.1); or, 'Out of the depths I cry to you, O LORD' (Ps. 130.1).

Furthermore, we would expect Jonah to show a bit of sorrow and to repent of his disobedience. Instead, the prayer of Jonah is neither a cry for help nor a prayer of repentance but is a prayer of thanksgiving, a formal composition that is fashioned after the danger has past. In contrast to the lament, which frames its address to God in present tense, the prayer (or psalm) of thanksgiving is composed in past tense. The worshiper recounts a situation of past distress and tells how God responded to prayer and brought deliverance. Examples of the prayer of thanksgiving are Psalms 30, 32, 40, 41, 107, and 116. Here Jonah prays but it is a formal prayer. Jonah's prayer may be from the gut of the fish, but it is not from the gut of Jonah.

In spite of the formal nature of Jonah's prayer, it is nevertheless quite powerful and moving in its depiction of his distress and his deliverance. He affirms that the LORD 'heard' him when he 'cried' from the belly of *sheol*. The word 'cry' is an earnest request for help and a plea for God to deliver. In light of the fact that *sheol*, the abode of the dead, sometimes symbolizes death itself (e.g. 1 Sam. 2.6; Ps. 18.5), the bringing back of a person from *sheol* is a metaphor that represents a near-death experience (Ps. 18.5; 30.3; 49.15; 86.13; and 116.3).

That Jonah cried out from *sheol* inclines some interpreters to insist that he actually died in the water. But inasmuch as Jonah does not state explicitly that he died, and considering the metaphorical nature of poetry, it seems more likely that the 'belly of *sheol*' represents the imminent death from which Jonah was saved.

Jonah acknowledges that although the sailors cast him into the sea, the LORD bears responsibility for the deed. 'You threw me into the deep', Jonah exclaims to God. Jonah knows that God is responsible. He does not blame the sailors for his trouble. God often uses human agents, situations, and circumstances to discipline his people. Are there times when we blame people for our troubles? We should emulate Jesus on the cross, who said of those who crucified him, 'Father, forgive them, for they do not know what they do'.

Jonah then expands on the extent of his suffering as he describes the sensation of being carried and tossed about by the 'current', the 'breakers' and the 'waves', all of which are under the control of the LORD.

Jonah now speaks in faith. At the beginning of Jonah's story, he had fled from the presence of the LORD; and now, ironically, he obtains the goal to which he had so foolishly aspired – he feels like he has been driven from the 'presence' of God. Yet Jonah, convinced that the LORD has heard his prayer (v. 2), declares confidently that he will return to the temple, that is, to the presence of God. In the midst of a hopeless situation, Jonah makes a statement of great faith – 'I will look again upon God's temple'. (Note. Some recent Bible versions translate this verse *incorrectly*, turning it into a question).

Three times in his psalm of thanksgiving, Jonah moves from a description of suffering to a confession of faith (vv. 4, 6 and 7). It is only in time of loss and need that we are able to return to what is truly valuable and important. If we are distant from God, we should attempt to return to his presence, and we should lay claim to the grace and mercy of God.

Jonah also shares his pain. In this verse Jonah describes more fully his struggle in the watery depths. The waters engulfed him to his 'life' (*nephesh*), meaning that his 'life' was near drowning; that is, he was about to die. Also, he felt imprisoned and shackled as the depths of the sea surrounded him and as sea weed wrapped around his head.

Jonah goes down. Sinking deeper and deeper in the sea, Jonah tells us that he went down 'to the foundations of the mountains'. In the first half of the book, Jonah's descent is conveyed through the repetition of the Hebrew word that means 'go down' (*yarad*). Jonah went down to Joppa (1.3); he went down into the ship (1.3); he went down into the recesses of the ship (1.5); and he went down to the foundations of the mountains (2.6). Yet when Jonah reached bottom, God brought him up from the pit (2.6) and placed him on dry land (2.10).

Jonah's situation looks hopeless. His fate seems to be final. He states that the 'bars' of the earth shut behind him 'forever', as if he were locked in a great prison cell. Once again, however, Jonah proclaims his deliverance. In spite of the great depths to which Jonah had fallen, the LORD has brought him up. In spite of the apparent unalterable finality of the situation, the LORD has delivered him. In spite of his imprisonment in the 'pit' (*shachat*), which is another symbol of death (Ps. 16.10; 30.9; 49.9), the LORD has saved him. Our situation may look hopeless, but God can save.

Jonah remembers God. At his lowest point of despair, Jonah sensed his life fading away. But then he 'remembered' the LORD; and although Jonah was far from Jerusalem, his prayer reached the LORD in his 'holy temple'. Jonah knows that the LORD is present even in the depths of the sea, but in Hebrew theology, the temple is the place of the LORD's special presence and the place from which the LORD goes forth to enact salvation (2 Chron. 7.12-18). No matter where we are, we can call upon God, and he will hear our cries. From the bottom of the sea, he will hear us. From the midst of despair, he will hear us.

Jonah rejects idolatry. In light of his experience, Jonah passes on a lesson to the hearers of his prayer. He rebukes those who practice vanities. The word 'vanities' refers to empty, vain practices (Jer. 2.5; 2 Kgs 17.15; Prov. 13.11), and by extension can refer to vain idols (Deut. 32.21). 'Their covenant loyalty' (*chesed*) is their faithful observation of covenant obligations (cf. Isa. 57.1; Neh. 13.14; 2 Chron. 32.32). Jonah insists, therefore, that those who would attend to empty pursuits or to vain idols are unfaithful in their covenant responsibilities to the LORD. Referring to the unfaithful as 'they', Jonah apparently does not include himself as one of the sinners. Nevertheless, although Jonah does not overtly confess his guilt, perhaps his rebuke subtly implies a confession. Perhaps he realizes that his rebellion against the LORD is a breach of his own covenant commitment.

Jonah promises to be faithful. Unlike those who would act unfaithfully, Jonah promises to serve the LORD with sacrifices and with the fulfillment of his vows. Jonah fully expects to return to Jerusalem where he will offer up to the LORD thanksgiving sacrifices and fulfill his vows. Apparently, when Jonah was in the water he had cried out to the LORD with a plea for deliverance, and he had made a promise to bring sacrifices or offerings to the temple (cf. Ps. 54.6; 116.17). The promise to offer sacrifices and the making of vows were commonly included in a cry for help. We are not told the content of Jonah's vows, and it is possible that his pledge to fulfill his vows (v. 9b) is a poetic repetition of his promise to offer sacrifices (v. 9a). That is, Jonah may be describing the one obligation with two different terms.

The thanksgiving prayer of Jonah ends with the powerful assertion that 'salvation is of the LORD'. The salvation of the LORD is a theme that appears throughout the Twelve Prophets. Consider, for example, the following declarations of the prophets. 'besides me there is no savior' (Hos. 13.4); 'I will wait for the God of my salvation' (Mic. 7.7; cf. Hab. 3.18); 'you came forth to save your people' (Hab. 3.13); 'he will save' (Zeph. 3.17); 'I will save my people' (Zech. 8.7; cf. 10.6; 12.7); 'I will save you' (Zech. 8.13); 'he brings salvation' (Zech. 9.9); and 'the LORD their God will save them' (Zech. 9.16).

Jonah's statement that 'salvation is of the LORD' also testifies to his own experience of the LORD's mercy and grace. Jonah had fled from the LORD, but still the LORD saved him. From the depths of the sea, the LORD had saved him. From the threshold of death, the LORD had saved him. Jonah had been powerless to halt the storm but 'salvation is of the LORD'. Jonah was unable to free himself from the grip of the sea, but 'salvation is of the LORD'. 'God could have given up on Jonah – let him drown, let him sulk, leave him to his self-centered existence. But God's grace persisted – calling, saving, calling again, leading, teaching, confronting – always in tough and unrelenting compassion', but 'salvation is of the LORD'. Here at the center of the book, Jonah's declaration foreshadows the LORD's salvation of Nineveh and highlights the central theological commitment of the book.

The salvation of Jonah brings to mind the words of the Psalmist. 'He brought me up out of the slimy pit, out of the miry clay, and he set my feet upon a rock, and established my pathway' (Ps. 40.2). I am also reminded of the New Testament examples of Peter and Paul. Even though he denied Christ, Peter was not cast off. God forgave him and restored him to fellowship. Paul admitted that he was the chief of sinners, but still God saved him and used him. Then there is the church at Corinth – Paul writes to them saying, 'Do you not know that the unrighteous will not inherit the kingdom of God? Do not be deceived: neither fornicators, nor idolaters, nor adulterers, nor effeminate, nor homosexuals, nor thieves, nor covetous, nor drunkards, nor revilers, nor swindlers, will inherit the kingdom of God. And such were some of you; but you were washed, but you were sanctified, but you were justified in the name of the Lord Jesus, and by the Spirit of our God' (1 Cor. 6.9-11). God's grace is able to reach down to the lowest of us and bring us up.

God Grants Jonah a Second Chance

¹⁰And the LORD spoke to the fish, and it vomited Jonah upon the dry land (Jonah 2.10).

As soon as Jonah finishes his prayer, the LORD speaks to the fish, which once again complies with the LORD's bidding. The fish regurgitates Jonah upon the dry land, placing the prophet back safely where he had started.

In light of the fact that the LORD's command to the fish comes immediately after Jonah's prayer makes it likely that the LORD is moved to action by the prayer. Apparently, God believes that Jonah is now ready to go to Nineveh.

Conclusion to Jonah 1-2

The first half of the book of Jonah (chs. 1–2) begins with a word from God and ends with a word from God. In God's first word, God commands Jonah to go to Nineveh (1.1), but Jonah disobeys. In God's second word, God commands the big fish to regurgitate Jonah (2.10), and the fish obeys. Between these two commands from God, we follow the pointless flight of the rebellious Jonah as he descends into the depths of despair and as God raises him up. The first half of the book concludes with the grace of God being extended to Jonah.

Connecting with Jonah

(Questions for discussion)

What are some ways that we stubbornly resist God, even when he is trying to point us in the right direction?

Can you think of a time when God intervened in your life miraculously in order to bring about his divine will?

In light of the fact that God does not automatically discard those who fail, what actions should the Church take to help restore the fallen?

How does the story of Jonah illustrate the teaching of Hebrews 12?

What does it take to make us pray?

Why do we sometimes blame other people for our troubles?

What are some ways that we find ourselves in the belly of a 'big fish'?

Would you share a time when you were in the midst of despair, with no answer in sight, but God heard your cries for help and delivered you?

Talk about a time when God pursued you and pressed you towards sanctification?

What if ... ?

(Creative and imaginative ideas)

What if we name a problem that seems impossible and begin to list the miraculous ways that God might solve the problem?

What if we plan a special worship service devoted especially to seeking God's intervention in situations that seem hopeless?

What if we make an effort to minister to someone who has run from God?

Now, come up with your own 'What if ... ?'

4

A Repentant City and a Merciful God: Jonah 3.1-10

Setting the Direction: Second Chances

What is it that pleases God the most? – our words that *promise* faithfulness or our actions that *demonstrate* faithfulness? Let us consider two examples. (1) Jesus told a parable about a farmer who asked his two sons to go and work in the field. One of the sons promised to go into the field, but he never went. The other son refused to obey but later repented and went to the field (Mt. 21.28-32). (2) On the night that Jesus was arrested and condemned, Peter denied his association with Jesus. He denied knowing Jesus. But Peter was forgiven and offered a second opportunity to be obedient. On the Day of Pentecost Peter was filled with the Holy Spirit and became a mighty witness for the LORD and a great leader in the Church. Peter, possibly reflecting upon his own experience writes that 'God is patient toward us, not willing that any should perish' (2 Pet. 3.9).

Because of his grace, God is willing to call to us more than once. God knows that we have issues, and he bears with us. He is patient and persistent. He comes to us again and again, drawing us to himself.

Discussion Starters

Share an experience in which you resisted an assignment but finally consented?

Discuss a time when you failed at something but then you were given a second chance?

Did you try harder the second time? Explain ...

In what areas are you in need today of a second chance to obey to God?

Hearing the Word of God

Introduction

After delivering Jonah from the belly of the fish, the LORD repeats his assignment. Jonah is commanded to go to Nineveh. We hope that Jonah has been transformed by his disciplinary experience. We hope that Jonah now trusts that the LORD knows what he is doing. We hope that Jonah will now obey joyfully, even though he may not fully understand the reasons for his assignment.

The New Opportunity for Obedience

¹And the Word of the LORD came to Jonah the second time, saying, ²'Arise! Go to Nineveh, that great city, and call out to it the message that I will speak to you' (Jonah 3.1-2).

God speaks again. As soon as the great fish regurgitates Jonah onto the dry land, the LORD speaks to him a second time. We are reminded of the LORD'S appearance to Elijah the 'second time' (1 Kgs 19.7) when Elijah had fled into the wilderness. Like Jonah, Elijah was aided by a divinely appointed animal; in Elijah's case it was a raven.

The story moves on very quickly. We are not told the location where Jonah was deposited upon the land, nor are we told his physical condition after emerging from the stomach of the big fish. We are not offered any justification for the storm or any reflection on the meaning of the fish. We are given no hint regarding the attitude of the LORD toward Jonah or vice versa. In light of his earlier prayer (2.9), we expect Jonah to offer a sacrifice (cf. the sailors, 1.16; and Noah, Gen. 8.20), but he does not do so. The lack of detail regarding Jonah's attitude and character leaves the hearer to question the degree of Jonah's spiritual transformation. Like the first call to Jonah, this second call is brief and to the point.

The LORD repeats his command to Jonah. This renewal of commission begins with words that are identical to the LORD's earlier assignment. 'Arise, go to Nineveh, that great city, and call out' (v. 2). The next part of the command, however, is a bit different from the first assignment. Whereas the LORD at first had told Jonah to preach to the 'evil' city of Nineveh (1.2), here he does not mention Nineveh's sin. Instead the LORD orders Jonah to preach 'the message that I will speak to you'. Furthermore, the LORD had earlier instructed Jonah to call out 'against' (*ʿal*) Nineveh, but now he tells Jonah to call out 'to' (*ʾel*) Nineveh, a modification that hints at leniency. Clearly, in both commissions Jonah's assignment is to go to Nineveh and preach the LORD's message. However, the command is altered just a bit, enough that we might wonder about the reasons for the changes. Perhaps the LORD has already begun to rethink his judgment. We are not told the content of the 'message' that Jonah is to 'call out' to Nineveh.

As a prophet of God, Jonah does not have the option of choosing the message or changing the message. Jonah is under the same rule as that which was given by the LORD to Moses. 'You shall not add to the word that I command you, neither shall you take away anything from it' (Deut. 4.2; cf. Rev. 22.18). His message is not his own; it is the LORD's message. The message of the prophet, like the message of the preacher of the Gospel, is 'not a human word but ... the word of God' (1 Thess. 2.13).

Without a word of response to the LORD, Jonah rises up and travels to Nineveh where he proclaims a message of impending doom. In essence, his message is 'The end is near'.

46 The Book of Jonah

The Short Sermon

> ³**And Jonah arose and went to Nineveh according to the Word of the LORD. Now Nineveh was an exceedingly great city, a three day journey across. ⁴And Jonah began to enter into the city, a day's journey; and he said, 'Yet forty days and Nineveh will be turned over' (Jonah 3.3-4) .**

Jonah finally obeys the Word of the LORD and goes to Nineveh. Like before, Jonah does not speak to God; he only acts. Therefore, we have no indication of his attitude towards his assignment. Instead of focusing on Jonah, the narrative points toward the immensity of his task. The great magnitude of Jonah's mission is reflected in the enormity of the city. Nineveh is so large that Jonah will need three days to carry his message through the city. Apparently, the work of Jonah will take some time and effort.

The words, 'exceedingly great city' (*'ir gedolah le'lohim*), carry a double meaning. The phrase could just as well be translated 'a great city belonging to God', a translation that should cause us to think differently about the city of Nineveh. Even a wicked city belongs to God and he cares deeply about what transpires there.

The Jews considered Jerusalem to be the 'city of God', but they also proclaimed that 'The earth belongs to the LORD and all that fills it, the world and all who dwell in it' (Pss. 24.1; 50.12; 89.11). If the LORD is creator of the sea and the dry land (Jonah 1.9), is he not sovereign over the entire world, and does he not have the right to claim any and every city as his own? When the Apostle Paul arrived in the wicked city of Corinth, he was afraid to preach the Gospel until God spoke to him saying, 'Do not be afraid ... because I have many people in this city' (Acts 18.9-10). We should carry the Gospel to Las Vegas saying, 'This is a great city of God'; and of Jakarta and Shanghai we should claim, 'This is a great city of God'. Of Lagos and Lima we should believe, 'This is a great city of God'; and of

Karachi, Cairo, and Moscow we should proclaim, 'This is a great city of God'. These cities can be saved by the Gospel.

When Jonah reaches Nineveh, he begins to work his way through the city, preaching a simple message of judgment: 'Yet forty days and Nineveh will be turned over!' Once again, the narrative of Jonah is not as simple as it sounds. First, it is surprising that Jonah does not use the standard prophetic messenger formula, 'Thus says the LORD'. In fact, he does not mention the name of the LORD at all. Is Jonah attempting to undercut his own message? How can the Ninevites repent if they do not know which God is threatening them?

Second, the Hebrew word that is translated, 'turned over' (*haphach*) can have a double meaning. The word is used to describe God's 'overthrow' of Sodom and Gomorrah (Gen. 19.25) and of Israel (Amos 4.11); but it can also mean to 'change direction', as in the turning around of a chariot (1 Kgs 22.34). It can mean to 'change' or 'transform' as in the changing of water to blood (Exod. 7.17) or the changing of Saul into a different man (1 Sam. 10.6, cf. Deut. 23.5; Jer. 31.13). It can refer to the changing of heart, loyalty, or allegiance as when the 'heart of Pharaoh turned' (Exod. 14.5; cf. Ps. 105.25), or when the LORD 'turned' against rebellious Israel (Isa. 63.10), or when Job laments, 'those whom I love have turned against me' (Job 19.19). Therefore, the message of Jonah could be translated, 'Yet forty days and Nineveh will turn around', or even 'Yet forty days and Nineveh will be converted'!

Although the narrative demonstrates that Jonah and the people of Nineveh interpret the prophecy in the negative sense of 'overthrown' rather than in the more positive sense of 'turned around' or 'converted', it is unnecessary to choose between the two meanings. Rather, the two meanings can be held together in a suspenseful tension that awaits resolution in the subsequent unfolding of the story. Viewed another way the two meanings can be interpreted as theological complements. Thus, the prophetic word both tears down and builds up (Jer. 1.10), wounds and heals. While the Word of the LORD challenges and overthrows the comfortable and self-sufficient, the overthrow can result in a positive process of transformation. The turning to God in repentance requires first the overturning of self-reliance, self-centeredness and self-righteousness. In sum, the prophetic word overturns, turns over, turns around, changes, converts, and transforms those who will hear it.

The Amazing Turn

> ⁵**And the Ninevites believed God, and they proclaimed a fast and put on sackcloth from the greatest of them to the least of them. ⁶And the matter reached the king of Nineveh, and he arose from his throne and removed his robes from on him, covered himself with sackcloth and sat in ashes. ⁷And he sent out a call and said in Nineveh, 'By the decree of the king and his nobles, neither humans nor animals, herd nor flock shall taste anything. They shall not feed nor drink water. ⁸And let them cover themselves with sackcloth, humans and animals, and let them cry mightily to God, and let them turn, each one from his evil way and from the violence that is in their hands. ⁹Who knows? God may turn and relent and turn from his burning anger and we will not be destroyed' (Jonah 3.5-9).**

It was noted earlier (Jonah 3.3) that Jonah would need three days to travel through the city and proclaim his message. After only one day, however, the entire city of Nineveh believes God and repents of their wickedness. God's word is powerful to change lives. Jonah's simple message is sufficient to touch the hearts of thousands of people.

Jonah's preaching generates a three-fold response from the people of Nineveh. First, they 'believed' God, a move that brings to mind the commitment of the patriarch Abraham (Gen. 6.15; Rom. 4.3), the Israelites in Egypt (Exod. 4.31) and the esteemed Daniel (6.23). Second, not satisfied to repent in word only, they 'proclaimed a fast'. Third, they 'put on sackcloth' as an outward sign of their heartfelt mourning. The practices of fasting and the wearing of sackcloth were common ancient Near Eastern expressions of sorrow and grief. The repentance of the Ninevites is not only immediate, it is comprehensive – every person from every layer of society participates in the acts of contrition. Everyone 'from the greatest of them to the least of them' repented (v. 5).

Furthermore, the king of Nineveh repents. When word of the events reaches the king of Nineveh, he lays aside his robes and sits in sackcloth and ashes. The urgent and unquestioning response of this foreign king is quite astonishing and unparalleled in the Bible. Contrast, for example, the stubborn response of Pharaoh to the mission of Moses (Exod. 5.1-2). Even Jonah, the Israelites, and their rulers do not compare favorably to Nineveh and her king when it comes to their responses to the prophetic word. It is easy to see how Jesus could say, 'The people of Nineveh will stand up with this generation at the judgment, and will condemn it because they repented at the preaching of Jonah; and behold, one greater than Jonah is here' (Mt. 12.41).

Moreover, the king proclaims a fast. Not only does the king demonstrate personal contrition, he is joined by his nobles in issuing a decree that the entire city should repent. The order appears to be unnecessary, since the people have already repented; but the decree, coming as it does from the ruler of the city, lends authority and legitimacy to the revival.

First, the king commands that both humans and animals should engage in a total fast, refraining from food and water. Second, the king orders that both humans and animals should put on sackcloth. The third and fourth commands, which do not mention the animals, require the people to 'cry mightily' to God and to 'turn' from their evil (*raʿah*) and violence (*hamas*). The Ninevites cry to 'God' (*ʾelohim*) rather than to 'the LORD' (*Yahweh*) perhaps because Jonah did not include the name of 'the LORD' in his preached message. In urging his people to repent, the king uses the word 'turn' (*shuv*), which in a covenantal context frequently signifies a change of loyalties, especially a return to God (e.g. Jer. 3.1; Hos. 6.1; Joel 2.12; Amos 4.6; Zech. 1.4; Mal. 3.7; cf. 1 Thess. 1.9). The actions specified in the decree combine to suggest sincere and authentic repentance on the part of the Ninevites. Let's look at the process of conversion in Nineveh. they believed; they repented (turned from violence); and they demonstrated their sincerity by fasting.

In his initial call to Jonah, the LORD had characterized Nineveh as an *evil* city, but now the king's decree describes the sin of Nineveh with a more specific term – violence. Nineveh was well-known as a vicious, sadistic, and merciless enemy of Israel. The king enjoins the people to turn away from this 'violence that is in their hands'.

Ironically, Israel herself is guilty of violence (e.g. Isa. 59.6); and the cities of Jerusalem (Jer. 6.7) and Samaria (Amos 3.10) are particularly guilty. Moreover, within the Twelve Prophets, Israel's violence is cited as a justification for the judgment of God (Mic. 6.12; Hab. 1.2, 3, 9; 2.8, 17; Zeph. 1.9; Mal. 2.16). The king's edict of repentance, therefore, applies to the Ninevites and to the Israelites and to us. In our day, violence is rampant. Consider the prevalence of child abuse, spouse abuse, teen violence, gang violence, and international concerns regarding human rights. The human race is no less violent than it was in Jonah's day.

The last part of the king's decree starts out with an exact quotation from the prophet Joel. 'Who knows? He may turn and relent' (Joel 2.14; cf. Mic. 7.19). In fact the whole scenario in Nineveh recalls Joel's call to Israel for repentance (Joel 2.12-14). Like Joel, the king uses the word 'turn' (*shuv*), hoping that Nineveh will turn away from her evil and that God will turn away from his anger (see Zech. 1.3). The king's desire for mercy is strengthened further by his suggestion that God may 're-lent' (*nacham*), a word that carries with it the connotation of 'regret' or 'sorrow' and is translated in some contexts as 'moved to pity' (Judg. 2.18). The King James Version translates it consistently as 'repent', even when God is the subject of the verb. The repentance of the Ninevites is aimed at moving God to pity so that he will change his mind and not destroy the city.

The God of Grace

¹⁰And God saw their actions, that they turned from their evil way. And God regretted the evil that he said he would do to them, and he did not do it (Jonah 3.10).

The repentance of Nineveh makes a deep impression upon the LORD. In a surprising turn of events, he responds to their change of heart with his own change of heart, choosing not to bring upon them the judgment that he had threatened.

Both the repentance of Nineveh and the repentance of the LORD are surprising to the us, because neither event could have been predicted from reading Jonah 1–2. The people of Nineveh 'turned' from their 'evil', and the LORD 'turned' from the 'evil' that he had planned to do to them. The word 'evil' (*ra'ah*) has the basic meaning of 'bad' or 'that which is harmful'. It can refer to moral evil, and it can refer to a disaster or a catastrophe, like the storm of chapter 1. The city of Nineveh, therefore, is 'evil' because she engaged in immoral aggressive actions that were harmful to other peoples. The storm of chapter one is sent by the LORD, but it is called 'evil' because it is a calamity that threatens to harm the sailors and their ship. Similarly, the LORD's planned judgment upon Nineveh is not morally evil, but it is called an 'evil' because it threatens to destroy the city.

In view of the fact that Jonah had promised the overturning of Nineveh in forty days, an event that apparently does not transpire, he might be vulnerable to the charge of false prophecy. However, two factors prevent such an indictment. First, as the foregoing discussion of Jonah 3.4 demonstrates, Jonah's prophecy is open to alternative interpretations. While Nineveh was not 'turned over' to destructive forces, it was 'turned over' in its attitudes and commitments. Second, the contingent nature of Hebrew prophecy allows God the freedom to adapt his plans in response to human actions. Earlier in the Bible, using many of the same terms found in the Jonah passage, the LORD says,

> At one moment I may speak concerning a nation or con-
> cerning a kingdom to uproot, to pull down, or to destroy it;
> but if that nation against which I have spoken turns (*shuv*)
> from its evil (*ra'ah*), then I will repent (*nacham*) concerning
> the evil (*ra'ah*) I planned to do to it (Jer. 18.7-8; cf. 26.3).

The LORD is free to express his anger toward human wickedness, but he is also free to change his anger to mercy.

Conclusion

The LORD's response to Nineveh's repentance should encourage the Church in at least two ways. First, if we should find
ourselves facing the displeasure of God (such as the churches
of Revelation 2–3), we must follow the example of Nineveh,
turning to God with all of our heart and believing that God will
forgive and restore us to his fellowship. Second, God's mercy
upon Nineveh should encourage the Church to be deeply involved in mission and evangelism both locally and globally. We
must believe that even the most wicked and depraved people
can be redeemed by the grace of God. Remember the words of
the Apostle Paul, 'Where sin abounded, grace abounded even
more' (Rom. 5.20). The worst sinners in the world can be
saved.

Connecting with Jonah

(Questions for discussion)

Have you ever been given a second chance? – at home, at work, by a friend?

Has God ever given you a second chance?

Are you in need today of a second chance to obey to God? In what area?

What task is facing you that is so enormous that it looks impossible?

Is there a city or a people that is so unchristian that we have given up hope for their salvation?

Consider the power of God's word to change lives. Share a testimony of your own transformation or that of a friend.

What is God's view towards violence in our society? on television? movies? between nations?

What does it take to make God change his mind?

Does our church need to repent like Nineveh (read Revelation 2-3)?

What if … ?

(Creative and imaginative ideas)

What if we identify specific sins in our lives and in the church and repent of those sins?

What if we name a city or a people for whom we have lost hope and we spend time in intercession for them?

What if we would plan or participate in a missions project that reaches out to a very evil city?

What if we would volunteer to assist the Teen Challenge ministry in our area?

Now, come up with your own 'What if … ?'

5

JONAH AND THE GOD OF GRACE: JONAH 4.1-11

Setting the Direction: Facing our Fears

A reality television show, called 'Intervention', tells the unhappy stories of people who have become unable to deal with their problems and to face up to life's challenges. These people have usually become addicted to drugs or alcohol. Often they have lost their jobs, their homes, and their children. The TV show recounts an 'intervention', which is the attempt of friends and loved ones to put enough concerted pressure on the troubled person to force that person into facing their problem and making a change for the better. This process of recovery involves the release of pent-up emotions, the expression of anger and hurt, the retelling of painful events, and the admission of faults and failures.

Although we may not have reached the point that we need an 'intervention' by our friends and family, we can find ourselves needing God's intervention. Temptations can become bondages, and hurt feelings can turn into deep anger. If we are to become whole in Christ, we must admit our hurts, face our fears, confess our faults, and pray for cleansing, healing, and deliverance.

Discussion Starters

Why do we bury our emotions and refuse to face up to our deep hurts and anger?

Stubborn attempts to escape painful feelings and to ignore the truth often leads to catastrophic consequences, such as depression, broken relationships, numbing addictions, and physical illness.

In what areas of our lives are we in need of an intervention by God? In the book of Jonah it is God himself who is intervening in the life of the prophet Jonah in order to press Jonah towards honesty and transparency. Jonah resists the process, but God persists to the end.

Hearing the Word of God

Introduction

In the previous lesson, we followed Jonah as he obeyed God and prophesied to Nineveh. In response to Jonah's preaching, the people of Nineveh turned to God, and in response to Nineveh's repentance God changed his mind and spared the city. At this point, therefore, the hearer might reasonably expect the story to conclude. The story, however, is not over, and God's pardon of Nineveh is not the climax because the story is not primarily about God and Nineveh but about God and Jonah. The concern of the story is not the Ninevites' evil, rather it is Jonah's misguided views towards God. In chapter 4, Jonah finally reveals his long hidden motive for fleeing his assignment, and the conflict between God and Jonah is pushed into the foreground.

Jonah's prayer of thanksgiving (2.1-9) had given us reason to hope that Jonah had changed, but he shows no evidence of transformation. Even though he believes that 'salvation is of the LORD' (Jonah 2.9), he does not want the LORD to save Nineveh. Jonah apparently cannot see Nineveh as anything more than a cruel and fierce enemy who had invaded Israel on a number of occasions, killing thousands of Israelites, burning villages and stealing many cattle.

Angry with God

> ¹But it was a great evil to Jonah, and he burned with anger. ²And he prayed to the LORD, and said, 'Please, O the LORD, is not this what I said while I was still in my own country? Therefore I proceeded to flee to Tarshish, because I knew that you are a gracious and compassionate God, slow to anger, and abundant in mercy, and relenting of the evil. ³And now, O the LORD, please take my life from me; because it is better for me to die than to live'. ⁴And the LORD said, 'Is it good for you to be angry?' ⁵And Jonah went out from the city, and sat down to the east of the city, and he made himself there a shelter, and sat under it in the shade, until he might see what would happen in the city (Jonah 4.1-5).

The LORD's forgiveness of Nineveh displeased Jonah greatly and he is very angry. The Hebrew word 'displeased' (*raʿah*) is translated 'evil' or 'bad' in earlier parts of Jonah. In a play on words, therefore, the forgiveness of Nineveh's evil is a 'great evil' to Jonah. Jonah's attitude may be quite surprising and shocking to the reader. If he is a prophet of God, how can Jonah have such a negative attitude toward the grace of God? If he knows God's reputation as a God of salvation (Jonah 2.10), then why does Jonah not give thanks to God for saving the people of Nineveh? The repentance of Nineveh and their salvation should have been an occasion for great celebration, so why is Jonah angry?

Although he is angry that Nineveh is saved, Jonah knows that the fate of Nineveh lies in the hands of the LORD; therefore, Jonah's anger is really directed at the LORD. Jonah does not question the validity of God's mercy; rather, he questions God's choice of Nineveh as the recipient of mercy. Because of his anger, Jonah does not come across as a heroic figure, especially when he is contrasted to earlier biblical characters such as

Abraham, who interceded intensely for Sodom and Gomorrah, cities whose wickedness was described similarly to that of Nineveh (Gen. 18.20-21; Jonah 1.2). We might also think of Moses, the greatest of all intercessors. When the LORD determined to destroy Israel, the prophet Moses intervened and pleaded for mercy (Exod. 32.1-14). Jonah, unlike Abraham and Moses, argues for punishment over mercy.

Throughout the story, the feelings of Jonah have remained hidden and his silence has been obvious. But now we finally learn what is on the mind of Jonah. He admits to God that he is angry and that he does not want the Ninevites to be saved. From the beginning Jonah had feared that God would be compassionate and forgive the evil Ninevites. Jonah had fled from his assignment not because he despises God's mercy. He believes in and appreciates God's mercy, it is part of his theology. He ran because he does not want God's mercy to be shown to the Ninevites. Jonah wants God to smite the enemy; he wants justice to prevail, but God hears Nineveh's prayers of repentance and his heart is touched by the humility of the Ninevites who fasted and prayed and mourned over their violence. God gives attention to those who are broken and contrite and who tremble at his word (Ezek. 18.23; Joel 2.32). There is rejoicing in heaven over one sinner that repents (Lk. 15.7).

Jonah knew that when he preached in Nineveh, the people would have an opportunity to be saved, but if he did not preach, then they would have no basis for repentance. That is why he ran from his assignment. Although Jonah was called to preach judgment, he knew that every proclamation of judgment includes within it an invitation to turn and be saved. Jonah ran away so that the Ninevites might not hear the prophecy and without the prophecy they will have no reason to turn, and if they did not turn, then God would send destruction and the Ninevites would perish. Jonah knew that the wrath of God is a temporary response to human evil, but that love and compassion are lasting, permanent attributes of God's holy character. Without sin, the wrath of God would never be seen; but the love of God is always evident. To support his theology, Jonah quotes a key text from Exodus, a text that recounts the personal revelation of the LORD to Moses. Moses was on Mount Sinai, and the LORD came down in a cloud and spoke to him saying:

> The LORD, the LORD God, compassionate and gracious, slow to anger, and abounding in steadfast love and faithfulness, keeping steadfast love for thousands, forgiving wrong and rebellion and sin, but he will certainly not acquit the guilty, placing the guilt of the fathers upon the children, and upon the children's children to the third and fourth generations (Exod. 34.6-7).

Jonah himself had preached about the grace and mercy of God. He had prophesied to King Jeroboam II that the king would be successful in spite of the fact that he was an evil king who showed no signs of repentance. God overlooked the evil in order to preserve Israel (2 Kgs 14.25-27). Now, however, Jonah is angry at God, who showed compassion on the city of Nineveh, which had repented from her wickedness.

Jonah, like Israel and like the Church, is more comfortable with God's punishment than with God's mercy. We are reminded of Jesus' parable of the workers (Mt. 20.1-16) in which an employer shows generosity to those who only worked for one hour of the day. We should also take a look at Jesus' parable about the Pharisee and the tax collector at the temple:

> And he spoke this parable to those who thought of themselves as righteous and who looked down on others. Two men went into the temple to pray; one was a Pharisee, and the other was a tax collector. The Pharisee stood and prayed, 'God, I thank you, that I am not like others who are extortioners, unrighteous, adulterers, or even like this tax collector. I fast two days of the week, and I give the tenth of all my possessions'. But the tax collector, standing at a distance, would not so much as lift up his eyes toward heaven, but beat on his chest, saying, 'God have mercy on me a sinner'. I tell you, this man went home justified rather than the

other: for whoever who exalts himself shall be brought low; and whoever humbles himself will be lifted up (Lk. 18.9-14).

We might also point to the parable of the prodigal son in which a loving father rejoices over the return of his lost child. These parables tell us that established religion always prefers justice over mercy, because justice is safe, predictable, controllable, and easily understood. Mercy is unpredictable, ambiguous, and leads to change. Jonah needs to hear Jesus say, 'love your enemies' (Mt. 5.43-47).

Look at the thief on the cross. He lived all of his life in sin, but with his last breath he asked for God's mercy, and God saved him. When we stand before God, he will not ask how *long* we served him. There are no second class citizens of heaven. Nineveh did not deserve God's grace, and neither do we! Yet God is a God of grace and mercy.

Like many of us, Jonah was resistant to change. He was not open to what God wanted to do in Nineveh! He probably thought to himself, 'We have never done it this way'. God was working; God was moving; but Jonah wanted no part of it. Many of us are not open to anything new and different. The early Pentecostal movement was rejected by the mainline churches because it was new and different. Later on, the Pentecostals rejected the charismatics for the same reasons. We should have learned by now that God is constantly doing a new thing in the world, and we need discernment to know what God is doing. It is important that we believe in the God of the Bible rather than a God of our own invention. Jonah was not ready to believe in a God of abundant grace who would save Israel's enemy.

Jonah is so angry that he prays to die. He no longer desires to live in a world where his enemies are offered redemption and where evil is so quickly pardoned. However, given Jonah's previous record of withholding information, it is not altogether clear whether his wish to die is genuine or whether it is a manipulative ploy to arouse the sympathy of the LORD (and the hearer?). Jonah's plea might be compared to similar cries from

Moses (Num. 11.15) and Elijah (1 Kgs 19.4), but the comparison does not elevate Jonah since he speaks not from a context of persecution and self-denial but from small-mindedness and hardness of heart.

Even though Jonah is clearly in the wrong, we must appreciate the freedom that God gives him to complain. God's people are not mindless pawns, pushed around by the decrees of the sovereign God. God allows us to vent our frustrations to him. God himself desires to hear what is on our mind, because our covenant with him is one of relationship, mutuality, and communion. God is our heavenly father, and he seeks to have fellowship with his children. If we do not understand what God is doing in our lives then we should bring those feelings to God in prayer. God knows our hearts, and he wants us to pour out our soul to him.

Jonah is not the first to wrestle with God. The list of wrestlers is astonishing, people who confronted God with his intents and actions. Abraham wrestled with God about Sodom. Moses argued with God about Israel. Gideon complained saying, 'God has deserted us'. Many of the Psalms ask the question 'Why?' Jeremiah was ready to quit preaching. Ezekiel's vision made him 'angry and bitter'. Both Amos and Habakkuk asked God, 'How long?' The entire book of Job is the story of one man's struggle to understand the actions of God. We could go on and on with this list. Do we have the right to wrestle? From the time that Jacob wrestled with God, and demanded to know God's name, the wrestling has continued. The wrestling shapes Jacob, wounding his hip joint, and changing his name. God continues to wrestle because we are formed in God's image and our identity is shaped in the wrestling. Our perception of the image of God partially determines our own self-image. We must wrestle with God in order to know God and to be like God.

'Is it good for you to be angry?' – the LORD responds to Jonah with a rhetorical question that is designed to draw him into a deeper conversation regarding his anger. God's personal engagement with Jonah demonstrates that God values Jonah as a person, not just as an instrument of prophecy. God takes seriously Jonah and his theological concerns.

Jonah once again retreats into stubborn silence and does not reply to the LORD's question. He apparently does not wish to continue the dialogue, nor does he seem to be appreciative of God's personal attention. Jonah withdraws from the LORD and from the city and builds himself a small shelter and sits in its shade, waiting to see what would happen in the city. Perhaps Jonah hopes that his complaint will cause the LORD to go back to his original plan of punishing Nineveh.

Like Jonah, we sometimes prefer solitude and silence. We sometimes are unwilling to deal with our feelings and our issues with God. Hiding from the truth, however, can lead to serious emotional problems and can result in addictive behavior that imprisons and controls our life.

God Defends His Grace

⁶**And the LORD God appointed a castor oil plant, and it grew up over Jonah, to be a shade over his head, to deliver him from his misery. And Jonah rejoiced greatly because of the castor oil plant. ⁷And God appointed a worm when the dawn came up the next day, and it attacked the castor oil plant and it dried up. ⁸And it came to pass, as soon as the sun rose, that God prepared a scorching east wind; and the sun attacked the head of Jonah, and he was overcome and asked that he might die. He said, 'My death would be better than my life'. ⁹And God said to Jonah, 'Is it good for you to be angry over the castor oil plant?' And he said, 'It is good for me to be angry, angry enough to die'. ¹⁰And the LORD said, 'As for you, you were deeply concerned over the castor oil plant, for which you did not labor, and which you did not make to grow; which came in a night and perished in a night. ¹¹So as for me, should I not be deeply concerned over the great city of Nineveh, in which there are more than one hundred twenty**

thousand persons that do not know their right hand from their left, and much cattle?' (Jonah 4.6-11)

Jonah continues to resist any dialogue with God, but God persists in reaching out to Jonah. The alternative to God's rebuke would be God's abandoning of Jonah, which would be even more devastating. Discipline is an expression of love, but abandonment is a radical expression of a broken relationship.

In this final episode of the Jonah story, God uses a plant, a worm, the wind and the sun to force Jonah out of his silence. Then God takes Jonah's own passions and turns them into the clinching argument that affirms God's concern for Nineveh.

In order to get to the root of Jonah's anger, God provides comfort to Jonah and then takes away that comfort. God appoints a plant to grow up over Jonah and provide him relief from the burning heat of the sun. The plant that grows up over Jonah is probably a castor oil bush, a poisonous plant that is common to the region and grows to heights of more than 20 feet with large leaves (2 ft. in diameter).

Ironically, the plant could be an answer to Jonah's death wish, since the plant was known to be poisonous (it was the plant from which the poison *ricin* is made). If Jonah had truly desired death, he could have eaten the leaves of the plant.

The large leaves of the plant shade Jonah from the heat of the sun and he rejoices 'greatly' because of the plant. Perhaps he regards the plant's miraculous appearance as a sign of the LORD's favor, or it could be that he rejoices simply in his new-found comfort. In any case, Jonah's joy is soon turned again to misery when, on the following morning, God appoints a worm to destroy the plant, thus taking away Jonah's shade. Then to add to Jonah's discomfort, God sends the scorching wind and the blazing sun. Without shelter, Jonah becomes so miserable that he again wishes to die. Jonah utters a despondent cry, 'My death would be better than my life'.

Through his giving of comfort to Jonah and then removing it, God attempts to bring Jonah's feelings to the surface. Then, once again God questions the validity of Jonah's anger. Jonah says, 'My death is good (*tov*)', and God replies, 'Is it good (*tov*) for you to be angry?' God, knowing that Jonah's death wish stems from his anger, compels Jonah to address the real issue, but Jonah insists that his anger is justified. According to psychologists, depression is often caused by the harboring of unexpressed anger. Jonah's silence and his wish to die are ways of avoiding his anger and frustration. Jonah is unwilling to cope with the situation.

Jonah's evil attitude toward the mercy of God demonstrates that the presence of charismatic gifts such as prophecy does not guarantee complete spiritual maturity. Any of us can be wrong! Prophets and other spiritual leaders are not immune to temptation of all sorts, and Jonah's anger proves that he has fallen headlong into sin. His anger is a result of his deep and shameful animosity toward the Ninevites.

When Jonah claims that his own feelings are justified, he unknowingly undermines his own position against God. The LORD seizes on Jonah's admission and through a rhetorical question he presses Jonah to face up to his passions. The LORD points out Jonah's deep concern (*chus*) for a plant that had grown up in one night and dried up in one night, a plant for which Jonah had invested neither time nor labor. The message is incisive – if Jonah is deeply concerned about a mere plant, then how can he condemn the LORD for being concerned about a city of 120,000 persons and their livestock? Jonah cares about the plant, but he does not care for the people of Nineveh. What do we care about? Do we care about *things* or do we care about *people*? Are we, like Martha, 'anxious and troubled about many things' (Lk. 10.41)?

The inhabitants of Nineveh are characterized by the LORD as 'human beings who do not know their right hand from their left', a description that may refer to the young children but which more likely describes figuratively the Ninevites lack of instruction in the laws of God and their lack of spiritual discernment. After all, if the metaphor had been intended as a description of innocent children, the writer could have used the word 'children' (*yeledim*) instead of the word 'human being' (*'adam*).

Earlier in the prophets, the Israelites, who were fully instructed in the ways of God and yet rebelled against him, sought and received the LORD'S pity (*chus*, Joel 2.17). Now in Jonah, the LORD implies that the Ninevites who 'do not know their right hand from their left hand' should not be denied the same benefit of grace.

The final words of the book of Jonah – 'and many cattle' – are puzzling. Why would the LORD mention his concern for the cattle? I would suggest four possible reasons: 1. the cattle fasted and wore sackcloth along with the humans (Jonah 3.7); 2. the cattle are more valuable than the castor oil plant that Jonah cares so much about; 3. the cattle represent the LORD'S concern for all of creation; and 4. the cattle register Jonah's resentment of the Ninevites. This last point, presented convincingly by Rickie Moore in his article '"And Also Much Cattle": Prophetic Passions and the End of Jonah', draws attention to the passions of Jonah which he is unwilling or unable to verbalize honestly. The LORD's mention of the cattle would remind Jonah of the violent Assyrian (Ninevite) incursions into Israel, which resulted in the capture and deportation of women, children, and livestock. Perhaps some of the cattle in Nineveh had been stolen from Israel! The LORD, therefore, provokes Jonah and forces him to acknowledge his animosity toward Nineveh. Until now, Jonah has acted but not constructively; he has prayed but not fervently, he has spoken but not forthrightly. The LORD will not allow Jonah to repress his feelings any longer.

The LORD's concern for the cattle brings to mind the teachings of Jesus, who said that God's eye is on the sparrow (Lk. 12.6), God feeds the ravens (Lk. 12.24), and God clothes the grass of the field (Lk. 12.28). If God cares for the sparrow, the raven, and the grass (and the cattle) how much more does he care for his people!

The Message of Jonah

Readers of the book of Jonah have observed in the story a number of vital motifs, including the following: 1. the futility of disobedience; 2. the sovereignty of God over creation; 3. the power of repentance; 4. God's freedom to show mercy to the wicked; 5. the contingency of prophetic predictions; and 6. God's concern for nations other than Israel. Among these important motifs, God's gracious response to repentance has long been regarded as a dominant theme of the story.

As important as these themes are, however, none of them is sufficient to encompass the entire book. The only motif that is present in every part of the story is the conflict between Jonah and God. Although the LORD's sending of Jonah to Nineveh provides the structure for the narrative of Jonah, the story goes beyond the salvation of Nineveh. From the first scene to the last, it is the tension between Jonah and God that is kept before the reader.

The turning point of the story is the surprising repentance of Nineveh followed by God's subsequent change of mind. Once God chooses to show mercy to the wicked Ninevites, the prophet becomes angry with God. God's forgiveness of Nineveh gives opportunity for Jonah to articulate his anger at God, an articulation that reveals the heart of Jonah and gets to the heart of the story. Jonah is furious at God's compassion, which the prophet regards as injustice. It is not that Jonah is opposed to the compassion of the LORD, but that Jonah is opposed to the LORD's showing compassion to Nineveh, a merciless enemy of Israel. Jonah prefers that God keep to his original pronouncement of judgment upon Nineveh. Jonah's theology tells him that God should not relent, because Nineveh is wicked and deserving of punishment.

The events surrounding Nineveh are just the setting for getting to the real issue, which is Jonah's theological struggle with God. There is not only something to be learned from Jonah's theology, which generates his anger, but there is also something to be learned from Jonah's experience, his experience of conflict with God. Jonah's story shows respect for passionate believing confrontation with God. Jonah, though an adult, is undergoing a re-education, a painful process of theological formation (sanctification), and he struggles against the yoke.

Conclusion

The book of Jonah focuses on the interrelationships between Jonah, the LORD, the sailors, and the Ninevites; yet the beauty of the story is that we may find ourselves in the place of any of the characters at a given time. We may be Jonah, questioning God, angry at God, wishing evil upon our enemies. Or, we may be the Ninevites, repenting of our sins and hoping that God will receive us mercifully. We may place ourselves in the role of the LORD, who is making every attempt to break through to a deeper level of communication with one of his children. At times we may be the sailors, who are caught up as unwilling participants in a larger drama that is shaped by the actions of others. In the end, we come face to face with the God of amazing Grace.

Connecting with Jonah

(Questions for discussion)

Share a time when you questioned God? Share a time when you were angry with God?

Do you rejoice when you see justice accomplished or do you prefer mercy?

How do you feel when God prospers wicked people?

Have you buried your emotional hurts and your anger? Is it hard for you to bring your feelings to God in prayer?

How should we respond to the failures of spiritual leaders?

Is your care for people greater than your care for your possessions? How do you demonstrate your care for people?

How do you react to change? – change in society, change in the church?

How can we demonstrate our openness to a new and different move of the Holy Spirit?

God cares for the sparrow, the raven, the grass, and the cattle – name a few ways that God shows his care for you.

What if ... ?

(Creative and imaginative ideas)

What if we take a sheet of paper and list our grievances against God – then present them honestly to God in prayer, trusting that he will give us peace?

What if we find a way to bless someone who does not deserve our blessing (Mt. 5.44)?

What if we sell some of our prized possessions and use the money to show our care of people (Lk. 18.22)?

What if we invite change in regard to our approach or method in some area of the church? What if we pray and ask God to show us the direction that he would have us to go?

Now, come up with your own 'What if ... ?'

Part II

Outlines and Handouts

OUTLINE 1

A DIFFICULT ASSIGNMENT AND A DANGEROUS CHOICE: JONAH 1.1-3

I. Introduction to the Book of Jonah

Everyone knows the story of Jonah and the whale – or big fish, as the book of Jonah puts it – but this episode in the life of Jonah carries deeper significance than we sometimes realize. Jonah is a rebellious prophet who refuses to complete the assignment that the LORD gives to him.

A. Overview of the Book of Jonah

The book of Jonah is set forth in two halves, and each of these halves begins with the same statement: 'The Word of the LORD came to Jonah' (1.1; 3.1).

B. Outline of the Book of Jonah

C. The Book of Jonah Is Different from Other Prophetic Books

1. Jonah is the only prophetic book that has no title or introduction.

2. Another characteristic that makes Jonah different is that Jonah is entirely a story about the prophet.

3. Another unique quality of Jonah is its unceasing intensity. Most everything in Jonah is big and intense. The Hebrew word 'big' (*gadol*) is found fourteen times in the book of Jonah.

4. Unlike the mission of other prophets, Jonah's assignment requires him to travel to a foreign country where he will deliver a message of judgment.

5. Jonah is given a second commission. Jonah is the only prophet who needed to have his assignment repeated a second time.

6. Jonah is the only prophet who does not mention God in his preaching.

II. A Difficult Assignment (1.1)

A. The first half of the book (chapters 1 and 2) tells of God's assignment to Jonah and Jonah's refusal to obey.

B. The difficult assignment causes tension between Jonah and God.

C. Jonah's Assignment comes by the Word of the Lord.

  1. The coming of the prophetic 'word' (*davar*) is a powerful revelatory experience in the life of a prophet.

  2. The Word of the Lord is sometimes visual.

  3. The Word of the Lord is more than speech or conversation; it is an event.

  4. The Word of the Lord is not Jonah's word; it is God's Word.

D. Like Jonah, we may be recipients of the Word of the Lord. Since the Day of Pentecost, the Church has been a Spirit-filled prophetic community that proclaims the message of Jesus.

III. The Assignment Is Given to Jonah

A. The name 'Jonah' ('dove') symbolizes gentleness and beauty (Song 5.2) and timidity (Hos. 11.11).

B. 'Amittai' means 'true' or 'faithful'; therefore, Jonah's name suggests that he might be a gentle, timid, but faithful prophet and that perhaps he will offer himself on behalf of others.

C. Jonah was an experienced prophet.

D. Jonah preached grace to a wicked king.

IV. Jonah's Assignment Is to Go to Nineveh (1.2)

A. Nineveh is a major city in the Assyrian Empire and a bitter enemy of Israel.

B. Although God spares Nineveh for a time, he would later execute complete judgment upon the wicked city.

C. Nineveh is the enemy, but Nineveh is not the real point of the story.

D. What is most important is the response by both God and Jonah to the repentance of Nineveh.

E. The Lord commands Jonah to 'arise, and go' to the big city of Nineveh and 'cry out' against it because of its evil.

F. The cries of the prophets are usually directed against the sins of Israel.

V. A Dangerous Decision (1.3)

A. For some reason, Jonah decides to disregard the clear command that God had given him. In an attempt to escape the 'presence of the Lord', he flees westward toward Tarshish instead of going eastward to Nineveh.

B. Although God lays upon his prophets a powerful calling, he does not force them into compliance. The message that is carried by the prophet is called a 'burden'.

C. Jonah resists his assignment, but that does not mean that he takes God lightly.

D. Jonah not only resists his assignment, he refuses to talk to God.

E. No other prophet refused their assignment like Jonah. Other prophets resisted God initially, but no other prophet turned and ran away.

F. Other prophets offer objections, but Jonah does not protest. Other prophets wrestle with God, but Jonah does not wrestle.

G. Jonah quickly found a ship that would take him away from his assignment. Jonah learned that disobedience comes easily for the one whose heart is rebellious.

H. Jonah's flight is highlighted in verse 3 by the repetition of the phrases 'to Tarshish' and 'from the presence of the Lord'.

I. Tarshish was as far from Nineveh as Jonah could go.

J. Why did Jonah make this dangerous choice to flee from his prophetic assignment? He must have had a strong reason for giving up his prophetic ministry and running to a city where he would have no friends, family, or church.

K. Can Jonah escape the presence of God? Of course not.

VI. Conclusion

Jonah was given a difficult assignment, and he chose to disobey. We too are faced with difficult choices.

OUTLINE 2

DISOBEDIENCE AND ITS STORMY EFFECTS: JONAH 1.4-16

I. Introduction

In the previous lesson, Jonah flees toward the distant city of Tarshish. In this lesson we follow Jonah as he attempts to escape the presence of the LORD.

II. Disobedience Brings Stormy Effects (1.4-5)

A. God hurls a mighty wind (*ruach*) that stirs up a raging storm, and the ship is in danger of sinking.

B. Several places in Scripture, the word 'tempest' is used as a symbol of God's anger and judgment (Jer. 23.19; Isa. 29.6).

C. Since Jonah refuses to talk to God, the storm is God's method of communication. Have you considered that the storm in your life may have been created by God himself? Throughout Scripture, God finds a multitude of ways to discipline and confront his erring children.

D. Jonah's disobedience endangers not only himself but also the sailors and their ship. It is clear that our disobedience to God results in misery and suffering not only to ourselves but also to others.

E. Jonah, however, is not yet suffering – he is asleep. He had gone down below deck to the remotest part of the ship, and had fallen into a deep sleep.

III. Disobedience Rebuked (1.6)

A. The ship is in danger, but Jonah sleeps. The captain of the ship does not understand how Jonah can sleep through the storm.

B. Jonah was sleeping during a time of confusion – the sailors were running to and fro trying to save the ship. Everyone was praying except Jonah.

C. Jonah was sleeping during a time of great danger – the ship was likely to sink. The storm was raging, but still Jonah slept.

D. Jonah was sleeping when he should have been awake. Of all people, he should have been awake and praying.

E. Our times require a praying church. Our times demand a church that is full of the Holy Spirit and power.

F. The captain pleads with Jonah to pray, but Jonah did not pray.

IV. Disobedience Revealed (1.7-10)

A. While the captain is busy rebuking the prophet, the ship's crew decides to cast lots in an effort to determine the cause of the storm.

B. The crew fire a volley of questions at Jonah, in order to learn more about the reasons for the storm.

C. Jonah seems willing to speak about God but still he is unwilling to speak to God.

D. Jonah's statement of faith, in spite of its brevity, is important in its content. The sea and the storm that is in the sea are in the Lord's control.

E. After Jonah says that he fears the Lord we read that the sailors 'feared greatly'; literally, 'they feared a great fear'.

F. Jonah tells the sailors; why does he refuse to tell the Lord?

G. Are there times when we talk to people, but we do not talk to God?

V. Disobedience Punished (1.11-16)

A. Jonah confessed that he is the cause of the storm; therefore, the ship's ask him, 'What must we do to you that the sea may be quiet for us?'

B. It is important that Jonah does not volunteer to leap or dive into the sea, for that would be suicide, an act that is strictly forbidden to the Jews. Jonah will not take responsibility for solving his own problem.

C. We must deal with our problems and not push them off onto someone else. Paul tells us that every one must carry their own load (Gal. 6.5).

D. Jonah is willing to die in his rebellion, but he is not willing to die to his rebellion. Jonah continues to be stubborn, even in the face of a life-threatening storm.

E. Even though Jonah asks the sailors to cast him overboard, they are unwilling to do so without first waging a renewed battle against the wind and waves.

F. The sailors quickly realize that they will be unable to reach the shore, and they cry out, 'Please, the Lord, please do not let us perish for taking this man's life, and do not lay upon us innocent blood'. It is ironic that the prophet stands by silently while the pagan sailors pray to the prophet's God.

G. Just as the Lord's hurling of the wind onto the sea generated the tempest, the crew's hurling of Jonah onto the sea caused the sea to stop its 'raging', a rage that symbolizes the anger of the Lord (Mic. 7.9).

H. The hypocrisy of Jonah is highlighted by the behavior of the sailors. It seems that we are being challenged to emulate these non-Israelite sailors rather than the Israelite prophet.

VI. Conclusion

Jonah's disobedience to God brought about a storm in his life that threatened not only Jonah but also those around him. In spite of the storm, Jonah continued to stubbornly resist God even to the point of dying in his rebellion. While the sailors called out to the LORD for help, the fleeing prophet kept silent and never prayed.

OUTLINE 3

A BIG FISH AND A SONG OF PRAISE:
JONAH 1.17-2.10

I. Introduction

In this third episode of Jonah's story, we learn of the three-day ordeal of Jonah within the belly of the fish (1.17–2.10). After three days in the belly of the fish, God commands the fish to regurgitate Jonah onto the dry land; and the fish obeys the Word of the LORD.

II. A Surprising Deliverance (1.17)

A. Since the death of Jonah is not the Lord's objective, he prepares a big fish to swallow Jonah, and to keep him from drowning. Jonah's story shows that in the face of rebellion God's grace pursues his servants and persists in calling them to mission.

B. In more ways than one, Jonah's confinement in the fish for 'three days and three nights' underscores the harshness of his ordeal from both a physical and emotional perspective.

C. While it is true that the fish saves Jonah from drowning, the fish itself is only a slightly less threatening environment than the open sea.

III. Deliverance Produces Thanksgiving (2.1-9)

A. Jonah speaks. The storm did not provoke Jonah to pray. The sailors could not force Jonah to pray; but from the stomach of the great fish, Jonah prays.

B. Jonah gives thanks. We expect to hear Jonah crying out to the Lord for help; but instead, we hear a prayer of thanksgiving that reports Jonah's cries after the fact.

C. In light of the fact that *sheol*, the abode of the dead, sometimes symbolizes death itself (e.g. 1 Sam. 2.6; Ps. 18.5), the bringing back of a person from *sheol* is a metaphor that represents a near-death experience (Pss. 18.5; 30.3; 49.15; 86.13; and 116.3).

D. Jonah acknowledges God's judgment. Jonah acknowledges that although the sailors cast him into the sea, the Lord bears responsibility for the deed. God often uses human agents, situations, and circumstances to discipline his people.

E. Jonah describes the sensation of being carried and tossed about by the 'current', the 'breakers' and the 'waves', all of which are under the control of the Lord.

F. Jonah speaks in faith. Jonah, convinced that the Lord has heard his prayer (v. 2), declares confidently that he will return to the temple, that is, to the presence of God. In the midst of a hopeless situation, Jonah makes a statement of great faith – 'I will look again upon God's temple'.

G. Jonah shares his pain. Jonah felt imprisoned and shackled as the depths of the sea surrounded him and as sea weed wrapped around his head.

H. Jonah goes down. Sinking deeper and deeper in the sea, Jonah tells us that he went down 'to the foundations of the mountains'. Yet when Jonah reached bottom, God brought him up from the pit (2.6) and placed him on dry land (2.10).

I. Jonah remembers God. At his lowest point of despair, Jonah 'remembered' the Lord; and although Jonah was far from Jerusalem, his prayer reached the Lord in his 'holy temple'.

J. Jonah rejects idolatry. In light of his experience, Jonah rebukes those who practice vanities. The word 'vanities' refers to empty, vain practices (Jer. 2.5; 2 Kgs 17.15; Prov. 13.11), and by extension can refer to vain idols (Deut. 32.21).

K. Jonah promises to be faithful. Unlike those who would act unfaithfully, Jonah promises to serve the Lord with sacrifices and with the fulfillment of his vows.

L. The thanksgiving prayer of Jonah ends with the powerful assertion that 'salvation is of the Lord'.

M. Jonah's statement that 'salvation is of the Lord' also testifies to his own experience of the Lord's mercy and grace. Jonah had fled from the Lord, but still the Lord saved him.

IV. God Grants Jonah a Second Chance (2.10)

A. As soon as Jonah finishes his prayer, the Lord speaks to the fish, which regurgitates Jonah upon the dry land.

B. The Lord is moved to action by Jonah's prayer. Apparently, God believes that Jonah is now ready to go to Nineveh.

V. Conclusion to Jonah 1-2

The first half of the book of Jonah (chs. 1–2) begins with a word from God and ends with a word from God. First, God commands Jonah to go to Nineveh (1.1), but Jonah disobeys; and second, God commands the big fish to regurgitate Jonah (2.10), and the fish obeys. Between these two commands from God, we follow the flight of the rebellious Jonah as he descends into the depths of despair and as God raises him up. The first half of the book concludes with the grace of God being extended to Jonah.

OUTLINE 4

A REPENTANT CITY AND A MERCIFUL GOD: JONAH 3.1-10

I. Introduction

After delivering Jonah from the belly of the fish, the LORD repeats his assignment. Jonah is commanded to go to Nineveh. We hope that Jonah has been transformed by his disciplinary experience. We hope that Jonah now trusts that the LORD knows what he is doing. We hope that Jonah will now obey joyfully, even though he may not fully understand the reasons for his assignment.

II. The New Opportunity for Obedience (3.1-2)

A. As soon as the great fish regurgitates Jonah onto the dry land, the Lord speaks to him a second time.

B. Jonah's assignment is repeated. The command is altered just a bit, enough that we might wonder about the reasons for the changes.

C. As a prophet of God, Jonah does not have the option of choosing the message or changing the message.

D. Without a word of response to the Lord, Jonah rises up and travels to Nineveh where he proclaims a message of impending doom. In essence, his message is 'The end is near'.

III. The Short Sermon (3.3-4)

A. Jonah goes to Nineveh. Like before, Jonah does not speak to God; he only acts. Therefore, we have no indication of his attitude towards his assignment.

B. The words, 'exceedingly great city' carry a double meaning. The phrase could just as well be translated 'a great city belonging to God'.

C. The Jews considered Jerusalem to be the 'city of God', but they also proclaimed that 'The earth belongs to the

Lord and all that fills it, the world and all who dwell in it'
(Pss. 24.1; 50.12; 89.11).

D. It is surprising that Jonah does not use the standard prophetic messenger formula, 'Thus says the Lord'. In fact,
he does not mention the name of the Lord at all.

E. The message of Jonah could be translated, 'Yet forty days
and Nineveh will turn around', or even 'Yet forty days
and Nineveh will be converted'!

IV. The Amazing Turn (3.5-9)

A. Nineveh repents. After only one day, the entire city of
Nineveh believes God and repents of their wickedness. God's word is powerful to change lives.

B. Jonah's preaching generates a three-fold response from
the people of Nineveh. First, they 'believed' God. Second, they 'proclaimed a fast'. Third, they 'put on sackcloth' as an outward sign of their heartfelt mourning.

C. The king of Nineveh repents. When word of the events
reaches the king of Nineveh, he lays aside his robes and
sits in sackcloth and ashes.

D. The king proclaims a fast. The decree of the king lends
authority and legitimacy to the revival.

E. Violence is confessed. The king orders the people to 'cry
mightily' to God and to 'turn' from their evil and violence.

F. In his initial call to Jonah, the Lord had characterized Nineveh as an evil city, but now the king's decree describes
the sin of Nineveh with a more specific term – violence.

G. The king's edict of repentance applies to the Ninevites
and to the Israelites and to us. In our day, violence is
rampant.

H. The king hopes for mercy. The repentance of the Ninevites is aimed at moving God to pity so that he will
change his mind and not destroy the city.

V. The God of Grace (3.10)

A. The Lord repents. The repentance of Nineveh makes a deep impression upon the Lord. In a surprising turn of events, he responds to their change of heart with his own change of heart, choosing not to bring upon them the judgment that he had threatened.

B. While Nineveh was not 'turned over' to destructive forces, it was 'turned over' in its attitudes and commitments. The Lord is free to express his anger toward human wickedness, but he is also free to change his anger to mercy.

VI. Conclusion

If we should find ourselves facing the displeasure of God (cf. the churches of Revelation 2–3), we must follow the example of Nineveh, turning to God with all of our heart and believing that God will forgive and restore us to his fellowship. Also, God's mercy upon Nineveh should encourage the Church to be deeply involved in mission and evangelism both locally and globally. We must believe that even the most wicked and depraved people can be redeemed by the grace of God.

OUTLINE 5

JONAH AND THE GOD OF GRACE: JONAH 4.1-11

I. Introduction
In chapter 4, Jonah finally reveals his long hidden motive for fleeing his assignment, and the conflict between God and Jonah is pushed into the foreground.

II. Angry with God (4.1-5)
A. The Lord's forgiveness of Nineveh displeased Jonah greatly and he is very angry.

B. Although he is angry that Nineveh is saved, Jonah knows that the fate of Nineveh lies in the hands of the Lord; therefore, Jonah's anger is really directed at the Lord.

C. Jonah wants God to smite the enemy; he wants justice to prevail, but God hears Nineveh's prayers of repentance and his heart is touched by the humility of the Ninevites who fasted and prayed and mourned over their violence.

D. Jonah knew that when he preached in Nineveh, the people would have an opportunity to be saved, but if he did not preach, then they would have no basis for repentance. That is why he ran from his assignment.

E. Jonah himself had preached about the grace and mercy of God. He had prophesied to King Jeroboam II that the king would be successful in spite of the fact that he was an evil king who showed no signs of repentance.

F. Jonah is more comfortable with God's punishment than with God's mercy.

G. Jesus' parables tell us that established religion always prefers justice over mercy, because justice is safe, predictable, controllable, and easily understood. Mercy is unpredictable, ambiguous, and leads to change.

H. Like many of us, Jonah was resistant to change. He was not open to what God wanted to do in Nineveh!

I. Jonah is so angry that he prays to die. He no longer desires to live in a world where his enemies are offered redemption and where evil is so quickly pardoned.

J. Even though Jonah is clearly in the wrong, we must appreciate the freedom that God gives him to complain.

K. Jonah is not the first to wrestle with God. We must wrestle with God in order to know God and to be like God.

L. God values Jonah as a person, not just as an instrument of prophecy. God takes seriously Jonah and his theological concerns.

M. Jonah does not wish to continue the dialogue, nor does he seem to be appreciative of God's personal attention.

III. God Defends His Grace (4.6-11)

A. Jonah continues to resist any dialogue with God, but God persists in reaching out to Jonah.

B. In order to get to the root of Jonah's anger, God provides comfort to Jonah and then takes away that comfort.

C. The large leaves of the plant shade Jonah from the heat of the sun and he rejoices 'greatly' because of the plant.

D. Once again God questions the validity of Jonah's anger. Jonah's silence and his wish to die are his way of avoiding his anger and frustration.

E. Jonah's evil attitude toward the mercy of God demonstrates that the presence of charismatic gifts such as prophecy does not guarantee complete spiritual maturity.

F. The message is clear – if Jonah is deeply concerned about a mere plant, then how can he condemn the Lord for being concerned about a city of 120,000 persons and their livestock?

G. The inhabitants of Nineveh are characterized by the Lord as 'human beings who do not know their right hand from their left', a description that may refer to the young children but which more likely describes figuratively the Ninevites lack of instruction in the laws of God and their lack of spiritual discernment.

H. The final words of the book of Jonah – 'and many cattle' – are puzzling. The Lord's mention of the cattle would remind Jonah of the violent Assyrian (Ninevite) incursions into Israel, which resulted in the capture and deportation of women, children and livestock.

I. If God cares for the sparrow, the raven and the grass – and the cattle – how much more does he care for his people!

IV. The Message of Jonah

A. God's gracious response to repentance has long been regarded as a dominant theme of the story.

B. The only motif that is present in every part of the story is the conflict between Jonah and God.

C. The events surrounding Nineveh are just the setting for getting to the real issue, which is Jonah's theological struggle with God. Jonah, though an adult, is undergoing a re-education, a painful process of theological formation (sanctification), and he struggles against the yoke.

V. Conclusion

The book of Jonah focuses on the interrelationships between Jonah, the LORD, the sailors and the Ninevites, yet the beauty of the story is that we may find ourselves in the place of any of the characters at a given time. In the end, we come face to face with the God of amazing Grace.

Handout 1

A Difficult Assignment and a Dangerous Choice: Jonah 1.1-3

I. Introduction to the Book of Jonah

Everyone knows the story of Jonah and the whale – or big fish, as the book of Jonah puts it – but this episode in the life of Jonah carries deeper significance than we sometimes realize. Jonah is a disobedient prophet who refuses to complete the assignment that the Lord gives to him.

A. Overview of the Book of Jonah
The book of Jonah is set forth in two halves; each begins with the same statement: 'The _____ of the Lord came to Jonah' (1.1; 3.1).

B. Outline of the Book of Jonah

C. The Book of Jonah Is _____ from Other Prophetic Books
1. Jonah is the only prophetic book that has no _____ or introduction.
2. Another characteristic that makes Jonah different is that Jonah is entirely a _____ about the prophet.
3. Another unique quality of Jonah is its unceasing intensity. Most everything in Jonah is _____ and intense. The Hebrew word 'big' (*gadol*) is found 14 times in the book of Jonah.
4. Unlike the mission of other prophets, Jonah's assignment requires him to travel to a _____ country where he will deliver a message of judgment.
5. Jonah is given a _____ commission. Jonah is the only prophet who needed to have his assignment repeated a second time.
6. Jonah is the only prophet who does not mention _____ in his preaching.

II. A Difficult Assignment (verse 1)

    A. The first half of the book (chapters 1 and 2) tells of God's assignment to Jonah and Jonah's _____ to obey.

    B. The difficult assignment causes _____ between Jonah and God.

    C. Jonah's Assignment comes by the _____ of the Lord.

        1. The coming of the prophetic 'word' (davar) is a powerful _____ experience in the life of a prophet. It is an encounter with the majesty and holiness of God.

        2. The Word of the Lord is sometimes _____.

        3. The Word of the Lord is more than speech or conversation; it is an _____.

        4. The Word of the Lord is not Jonah's word; it is God's Word. The Word does not _____ in Jonah, and he does not own it or control it.

    D. Like Jonah, we may be recipients of the Word of the Lord. Since the Day of Pentecost, the Church has been a Spirit-filled _____ community that proclaims the message of Jesus.

III. The Assignment Is Given to Jonah

    A. The name 'Jonah' ('dove') symbolizes _____ and beauty (Song 5.2) and timidity (Hos. 11.11).

    B. 'Amittai' means 'true' or 'faithful'; therefore, Jonah's name suggests that he might be a _____, timid, but faithful prophet and that perhaps he will offer himself on behalf of others.

    C. Jonah was an _____ prophet.

    D. Jonah preached _____ to a wicked king.

IV. Jonah's Assignment Is to Go to Nineveh (verse 2)

    A. Nineveh is a major city in the _____ Empire and a bitter enemy of Israel.

B. Although God spares _____ for a time, he would later execute complete judgment upon the wicked city.

C. Nineveh is the _____, but Nineveh is not the real point of the story.

D. What is most important in the book of Jonah is the _____ by both God and Jonah to the repentance of Nineveh.

E. The Lord commands Jonah to 'arise, and go' to the big city of Nineveh and 'cry out' against it because of its

_____.

F. The cries of the prophets are usually directed against the sins of _____.

V. A Dangerous Decision (verse 3)

A. For some reason, Jonah decides to _____ the clear command that God had given him. In an attempt to escape the 'presence of the Lord', he flees westward toward Nineveh instead of going eastward to Nineveh.

B. Although God lays upon his prophets a powerful calling, he does not force them into compliance. The message that is carried by the prophet is called a

_____.

C. Jonah _____ his assignment, but that does not mean that he takes God lightly.

D. Jonah not only resists his assignment, he refuses to _____ to God.

E. No other prophet _____ their assignment like Jonah. Other prophets resisted God initially, but no other prophet turned and ran away.

F. Other prophets offer _____, but Jonah does not protest. Other prophets wrestled with God, but Jonah does not wrestle.

G. Jonah quickly found a ship that would take him away from his assignment. Jonah learned that _____ comes easily for the one whose heart is rebellious.

H. Jonah's flight is highlighted in verse 3 by the repetition
of the phrases _____ and 'from
the presence of the Lord'.

I. Tarshish was as far from _____ as Jonah
could go.

J. Why did Jonah make this dangerous choice to
_____ from his prophetic assignment?

K. Can Jonah _____ the presence of God?
Of course not.

VI. Conclusion

Jonah was given a difficult assignment, and he chose to disobey. We too are faced with difficult choices. What path will
we choose?

HANDOUT 2

DISOBEDIENCE AND ITS STORMY EFFECTS: JONAH 1.4-16

I. Introduction
In the previous lesson, Jonah flees toward the distant city of _____. In this lesson we follow Jonah as he attempts to escape the presence of the LORD.

II. Disobedience Brings Stormy Effects (1.4-5)
A. God hurls a mighty _____ that stirs up a raging storm, and the ship is in danger of sinking.

B. Several places in Scripture, the word 'tempest' is used as a symbol of God's _____ and judgment (Jer. 23.19; Isa. 29.6).

C. Since Jonah refuses to talk to God, the _____ is God's method of communication. Have you considered that the storm in your life may have been created by God himself? Throughout Scripture, God finds a multitude of ways to discipline and confront his erring children.

D. Jonah's disobedience endangers not only himself but also the sailors and their ship. It is clear that our _____ to God results in misery and suffering not only to ourselves but also to others.

E. Jonah, however, is not yet suffering – he is _____. He had gone down below deck to the remotest part of the ship, and had fallen into a deep sleep.

III. Disobedience Rebuked (1.6)
A. The ship is in danger, but Jonah sleeps. The captain of the ship does not understand how Jonah can _____ through the storm.

B. Jonah was sleeping during a time of _____.
The sailors were running to and fro trying to save the
ship. Everyone was praying except Jonah.

C. Jonah was sleeping during a time of great
_____ – the ship was likely to sink. The
storm was raging, but still Jonah slept.

D. Jonah was sleeping when he should have been
_____. Of all people, he should have been
awake and praying.

E. Our times require a _____ church. Our
times demand a church that is full of the Holy Spirit and
power.

F. The captain pleads with Jonah to _____, but
Jonah did not pray.

IV. Disobedience Revealed (1.7-10)

A. While the captain is busy rebuking the prophet, the ship's
crew decides to cast lots in an effort to determine the
_____ of the storm.

B. The crew fire a volley of questions at Jonah, in order to
learn more about the reasons for the
_____.

C. Jonah seems willing to speak _____ God but
still he is unwilling to speak to God.

D. Jonah's statement of faith, in spite of its brevity, is important in its content. The sea and the storm that is in
the sea are in the Lord's _____.

E. After Jonah says that he fears the Lord we read that the
sailors 'feared _____'; literally, 'they feared a
great fear'.

F. Jonah tells the sailors; why does he refuse to
_____ the Lord?

G. Are there times when we _____ to people, but
we do not talk to God?

V. Disobedience Punished (1.11-16)

A. Jonah confessed that he is the cause of the
_____; and the ship's crew ask him, 'What
must we do to you that the sea may be quiet for us?'

B. It is important that Jonah does not
_____ to leap or dive into the sea,
for that would be suicide, an act that is strictly forbidden
to the Jews. Jonah will not take responsibility for solving
his own problem.

C. We must deal with our _____ and not
push them off onto someone else. Paul tells us that every
one must carry their own load (Gal. 6.5).

D. Jonah is willing to die in his rebellion, but he is not willing to die to his rebellion. Jonah continues to be
_____, even in the face of a life-
threatening storm.

E. Even though Jonah asks the sailors to cast him overboard, they are _____ to do so with-
out first waging a renewed battle against the wind and
waves.

F. The sailors quickly realize that they will be
_____ to reach the shore, and they cry out,
'Please, the Lord, please do not let us perish for taking
this man's life, and do not lay upon us innocent
blood'. It is ironic that the prophet stands by silently
while the pagan sailors pray to the prophet's God.

G. Just as the Lord's hurling of the _____ onto
the sea generated the tempest, the crew's hurling of Jonah onto the sea caused the sea to stop its 'raging', a rage
that symbolizes the anger of the Lord (Mic. 7.9).

H. The _____ of Jonah is highlighted by the
behavior of the sailors. It seems that we are being challenged to emulate these non-Israelite sailors rather than
the Israelite prophet.

VI. Conclusion

In spite of the storm, Jonah continued stubbornly to
_____ God even to the point of dying in his rebellion. While the sailors called out to the LORD for help,
the fleeing prophet kept silent and never prayed.

HANDOUT 3

A BIG FISH AND A SONG OF PRAISE: JONAH 1.17-2.10

I. Introduction

In this third episode of Jonah's story, we learn of the three-day ordeal of Jonah within the belly of the fish (1.17–2.10). After three days in the belly of the fish, God commands the fish to regurgitate Jonah onto the dry land; and the fish obeys the Word of the LORD.

II. A Surprising Deliverance (1.17)

A. Since the _____ of Jonah is not the Lord's objective, he prepares a big fish to swallow Jonah, and to keep him from drowning.

B. In more ways than one, Jonah's confinement in the fish for 'three days and three nights' underscores the _____ of his ordeal from both a physical and emotional perspective.

C While it is true that the fish saves Jonah from drowning, the fish itself is only a slightly less _____ environment than the open sea.

III. Deliverance Produces Thanksgiving (2.1-9)

A. Jonah speaks. The storm did not provoke Jonah to _____. The sailors could not force Jonah to pray; but from the stomach of the great fish, Jonah prays.

B. Jonah gives thanks. We expect to hear Jonah crying out to the Lord for help; but instead, we hear a prayer of _____ that reports Jonah's cries after the fact.

C. In light of the fact that *sheol*, the abode of the dead, sometimes symbolizes death itself (e.g. 1 Sam. 2.6; Ps. 18.5), the bringing back of a person from *sheol* is a metaphor that represents a _____ experience (Pss. 18.5; 30.3; 49.15; 86.13; and 116.3).

D. Jonah acknowledges that although the sailors cast him into the sea, the Lord bears _____ for the deed.

E. Jonah describes the sensation of being carried and tossed about by the 'current', the 'breakers' and the 'waves', all of which are under the _____ of the Lord.

F. Jonah, convinced that the Lord has heard his prayer (v. 2), declares confidently that he will _____ to the temple, that is, to the presence of God. In the midst of a hopeless situation, Jonah makes a statement of great faith – 'I will look again upon God's temple'.

G. Jonah shares his pain. Jonah felt _____ and shackled as the depths of the sea surrounded him and as sea weed wrapped around his head.

H. Jonah goes down. Sinking deeper and deeper in the sea, Jonah tells us that he went down 'to the _____ of the mountains'. Yet when Jonah reached bottom, God brought him up from the pit (2.6) and placed him on dry land (2.10).

I. Jonah remembers God. At his lowest point of despair, Jonah '_____' the Lord; and although Jonah was far from Jerusalem, his prayer reached the Lord in his 'holy temple'.

J. Jonah rejects idolatry. In light of his experience, Jonah rebukes those who practice _____. The word 'vanities' refers to empty, vain practices (Jer. 2.5; 2 Kgs 17.15; Prov. 13.11), and by extension can refer to vain idols (Deut. 32.21).

K. Jonah promises to be faithful. Unlike those who would act unfaithfully, Jonah promises to serve the Lord with _____ and with the fulfillment of his vows.

L. The thanksgiving prayer of Jonah ends with the powerful assertion that '_____ is of the Lord'.

M. Jonah's statement that 'salvation is of the Lord' also testifies to his own experience of the Lord's mercy and
_____. Jonah had fled from the Lord, but still
the Lord saved him.

IV. God Grants Jonah a Second Chance (2.10)

A. As soon as Jonah finishes his prayer, the Lord speaks to
the fish, which _____ Jonah
upon the dry land.

B. The Lord is moved to action by Jonah's prayer. Apparently, God believes that Jonah is now ready to go to

_____.

V. Conclusion to Jonah 1-2

The first half of the book of Jonah (chs. 1–2) begins with a
word from God and ends with a word from God. First,
God commands Jonah to go to Nineveh (1.1), but Jonah
disobeys; and second, God commands the big fish to regurgitate Jonah (2.10), and the fish obeys. Between these two
commands from God, we follow the flight of the rebellious
Jonah as he descends into the depths of despair and as God
raises him up. The first half of the book concludes with the
grace of God being extended to Jonah.

HANDOUT 4

A REPENTANT CITY AND A MERCIFUL GOD: JONAH 3.1-10

I. Introduction

After delivering Jonah from the belly of the fish, the LORD repeats his assignment. Jonah is commanded to go to Nineveh. We hope that Jonah has been transformed by his disciplinary experience. We hope that Jonah now trusts that the LORD knows what he is doing. We hope that Jonah will now obey joyfully, even though he may not fully understand the reasons for his assignment.

II. The New Opportunity for Obedience (3.1-2)

A. God speaks again. As soon as the great fish vomits Jonah onto the dry land, the Lord _____ to him a second time.

B. Jonah's assignment is repeated. The command is altered just a bit, enough that we might wonder the about the _____ for the changes.

C. As a prophet of God, Jonah does not have the option of choosing the _____ or changing the message.

D. Without a word of _____ to the Lord, Jonah rises up and travels to Nineveh where he proclaims a message of impending doom. In essence, his message is 'The end is near'.

III. The Short Sermon (3.3-4)

A. Jonah goes to Nineveh. Like before, Jonah does not speak to God; he only acts. Therefore, we have no indication of his _____ towards his assignment.

B. The words, 'exceedingly great city', carry a double meaning. The phrase could just as well be translated 'a great city _____ to God'.

(Pss. 24.1; 50.12; 89.11).

_____'. In fact, he does not mention the name of the

Lord at all.

E. The message of Jonah could be translated, 'Yet forty days

IV. The Amazing Turn (3.5-9)

A. Nineveh repents. After only one day, the entire city of

Nineveh _____ God and repents of

B. Jonah's preaching generates a _____

C. The king of Nineveh repents. When word of the events

_____ and sits in sackcloth and ashes.

D. The king proclaims a fast. The decree of the king lends

E. Violence is confessed. The king orders the people to 'cry

_____ and violence.

F. In his initial call to Jonah, the Lord had characterized Ni-

neveh as an evil city, but now the king's decree describes

G. The king's edict of repentance applies to the Ninevites

H. The king hopes for mercy. The repentance of the Nine-

vites is aimed at moving God to pity so that he will

V. The God of Grace (3.10)

A. The Lord repents. The _____ of Nineveh makes a deep impression upon the Lord. In a surprising turn of events, he responds to their change of heart with his own change of heart, choosing not to bring upon them the judgment that he had threatened.

B. While Nineveh was not 'turned over' to destruction, it was 'turned over' in its attitudes and commitments. The Lord is free to express his anger toward human wickedness, but he is also free to change his anger to

_____.

VI. Conclusion

If we should find ourselves facing the displeasure of God (cf. the churches of Revelation 2–3), we must follow the example of Nineveh, turning to God with all of our heart and believing that God will forgive and restore us to his fellowship. Also, God's mercy upon Nineveh should encourage the Church to be involved deeply in mission and evangelism both locally and globally. We must believe that even the most wicked and depraved people can be redeemed by the grace of God.

HANDOUT 5

JONAH AND THE GOD OF GRACE: JONAH 4.1-11

I. Introduction

The concern of the story is not the Ninevites' evil, rather it is Jonah's misguided views towards God. In chapter 4, Jonah finally reveals his long hidden motive for fleeing his assignment, and the conflict between God and Jonah is pushed into the foreground.

II. Angry with God (4.1-5)

A. The Lord's forgiveness of Nineveh _____ Jonah greatly and he is very angry.

B. Although he is angry that Nineveh is saved, Jonah knows that the fate of Nineveh lies in the hands of the _____; therefore, Jonah's anger is really directed at the Lord.

C. Jonah wants God to smite the enemy; he wants _____ to prevail, but God hears Nineveh's prayers of repentance and his heart is touched by the humility of the Ninevites who fasted and prayed and mourned over their violence.

D. Jonah knew that when he preached in Nineveh, the people would have an opportunity to be saved, but if he did not preach, they would have no basis for repentance. That is why he _____ from his assignment.

E. Jonah himself had preached about the _____ and mercy of God.

F. Jonah is more _____ with God's punishment than with God's mercy.

G. Jesus' parables tell us that established religion prefers _____ over mercy, because justice is safe, predictable, controllable, and easily understood. Mercy is unpredictable, ambiguous, and leads to change.

H. Like many of us, Jonah was resistant to
_____. He was not open to what God
wanted to do in Nineveh!

I. Jonah is so angry that he prays to _____. He no longer desires to live in a world where his enemies are offered redemption and where evil is so quickly pardoned.

J. Even though Jonah is clearly in the wrong, we must appreciate the _____ that God gives him to
complain.

K. Jonah is not the first to _____ with
God. We must wrestle with God in order to know God
and to be like God.

L. God values Jonah as a _____, not just as an instrument of prophecy. God takes seriously Jonah and his
theological concerns.

M. Jonah does not wish to _____ the dialogue with God, nor does he seem to be appreciative of
God's personal attention.

III. God Defends His Grace (4.6-11)

A. Jonah continues to resist any dialogue with God, but
God _____ in reaching out to Jonah.

B. In order to get to the root of Jonah's anger, God provides _____ to Jonah and then takes away
that comfort.

C. The large leaves of the plant shade Jonah from the
_____ of the sun and he rejoices 'greatly' because of the plant.

D. Once again God questions the _____ of
Jonah's anger. Jonah's silence and his wish to die are way
of avoiding his anger and frustration.

E. Jonah's evil attitude toward the _____ of
God demonstrates that the presence of charismatic gifts
such as prophecy does not guarantee complete spiritual
maturity.

F. If Jonah is deeply concerned about a plant, then how can he _____ the Lord for being concerned about a city of 120,000 persons and their livestock?

G. The inhabitants of Nineveh are characterized by the Lord as 'human beings who do not know their right hand from their left', a description that may refer to the young children but which more likely describes figuratively the Ninevites lack of _____ in the laws of God and their lack of spiritual discernment.

H. The final words of the book of Jonah – 'and many _____' – are puzzling. The Lord's mention of the cattle would remind Jonah of the violent Assyrian (Ninevite) incursions into Israel.

I. If God cares for the sparrow, the raven, the grass, and the cattle, how much more does he _____ for his people!

IV. The Message of Jonah

A. God's gracious response to _____ has long been regarded as a dominant theme of the story.

B. The only motif that is present in every part of the story is the _____ between Jonah and God.

C. The real issue is Jonah's theological struggle with _____. Jonah, though an adult, is undergoing a re-education, a painful process of theological formation (sanctification), and he rebels against the yoke.

V. Conclusion

The book of Jonah focuses on the interrelationships between Jonah, the LORD, the sailors and the Ninevites, yet the beauty of the story is that we may find ourselves in the place of any of the characters at a given time. In the end, we come face to face with the God of amazing Grace.

RESOURCES FOR FURTHER STUDY

Allen, Leslie C., *The Books of Joel, Obadiah, Jonah, and Micah* (The New International Commentary on the Old Testament; Grand Rapids, MI: Eerdmans, 1976).

Fretheim, Terence E., *The Message of Jonah: A Theological Commentary* (Minneapolis, MN: Augsburg Pub. House, 1977).

Knight, George A.F., and Friedemann W. Golka, *Revelation of God* (International Theological Commentary; Grand Rapids, MI: Eerdmans, 1988).

Martin, Lee Roy, 'Jonah'. In *The Pentecostal Commentary on the Twelve* (Blandford Forum, UK: Deo Publishers, forthcoming).

Martin, Lee Roy, 'Jonah's Big Problem', *Church of God Evangel* (April 2008), pp. 12-13.

Moore, Rick D., "And Also Much Cattle': Prophetic Passions and the End of Jonah', *Journal of Pentecostal Theology* 11 (Oct. 1997), pp. 35-48.

Nixon, Rosemary A., *The Message of Jonah: Presence in the Storm* (The Bible Speaks Today; Downers Grove, IL: InterVarsity Press, 2003).

Index of Biblical References

Made in the USA
Columbia, SC
04 August 2024

39534583R00074